THE
WORLD *Mythology*
SERIES

KINGS,
GODS & SPIRITS
from
AFRICAN MYTHOLOGY

KINGS,
GODS & SPIRITS
from
AFRICAN MYTHOLOGY

TEXT BY JAN KNAPPERT

ILLUSTRATIONS BY FRANCESCA PELIZZOLI

Peter Lowe

British Library Cataloguing
in Publication Data
Knappert, Jan
  Kings, gods and spirits
  from African mythology.
  1. Tales-Africa
  2. Legends-Africa
  I. Title
  II. Pelizzoli, Francesca
  398.2′096 PZ8.1

ISBN 0 85654 051 X
Printed in Italy by
Grafiche Editoriale Padane

THE AUTHOR

Jan Knappert teaches at the School of Oriental and African Studies, London and has worked in and travelled widely throughout Africa conducting extensive research in Kenya and Tanzania. He is a leading expert on the languages and traditional folklore of Africa, especially Swahili, and has personally made extensive collections of myths and folk tales.

THE ARTIST

Francesca Pelizzoli graduated from Wimbledon School of Art in 1984 with special distinction in Illustration and Film. She gained first prize in the 1984 Thames Television Design Bursary and won first prize in the *Reader's Digest* 'Young Illustrator of the Year' competition as well as being a joint winner in 1985. She is now working as a freelance illustrator.

Contents

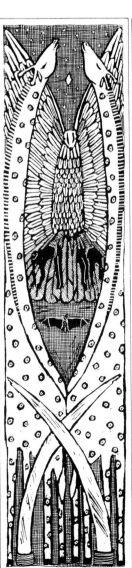

R. SENEGAL

R. NIGER

SAHARA DESERT

L. CHAD

R. LOGONE

R. NILE

RED SEA

R. SCEBELI

R. JUBA

R. CONGO

L. VICTORIA

L. TANGANYIKA

R. KWANGO

L. MALAWI

ATLANTIC
OCEAN

INDIAN
OCEAN

R. ZAMBEZI

KALAHARI
DESERT

R. LIMPOPO

R. ORANJE

Africa and its people

Africa is very large: 30 million square kilometres, three times larger than Europe, 22% of the total land mass of the Earth, yet it contains only about 9% of the total world population, less than 400 million people. One reason for this is that much of the land is desert, inhabited only by nomadic peoples who have learned to survive in its hostile conditions.

The Sahara, that vast ocean of sand, has an area of 10 million square miles, the size of China and there are many others—the Kalahari in the south, the Namib, the Nubian, Turkana and Somali deserts. South of the Sahara there is the Sahel, the 'sandy belt' where some grass and shrubs can grow but where the land is soon exhausted by grazing and a square mile is needed to feed one cow. The people are nomads, trekking from one arid area to another with their herds of cattle and flocks of goats, constantly moving south to stay ahead of the inexorable southward expansion of the Sahara.

In the centre of Africa, in Zaire, Uganda, Congo, Gabon, Cameroun and the Atlantic coast as far as Sierra Leone, the tropical forest grew to a height of a hundred feet or more. In many areas this primeval forest has been cut and burned to clear the land for food but there is still an impressive area of ancient forest left, for the time being. It is the home of many rare but splendid animals: the pygmy hippopotamus, the okapi, the gorilla, the chimpanzee, the leopard, the pygmy antelope or duiker, the Congo peacock, the red buffalo and numerous species of birds, reptiles and fishes occur only there.

The peoples who have settled in the forest remain there in very small communities, not more than a few hundred in a village. Many have been there for a very long time, centuries pass without them mixing with any other group. Each isolated group has developed into a tribe with its own language and its own religion. In many places they have burned down the forest completely so they can actually see the smoke of their neighbours, but they retain their own identity, their language and often their ethnic purity for few want their daughters to marry strangers with wrong religions and odd customs.

Most of the rest of Africa is covered by the savannah, a grassy plain, sometimes flat, sometimes undulating, sometimes swampy, mostly dry and dusty. This vast plain stretches from the Gambia and Senegal in the west across West Africa between the arid Sahel and the lush forest through the Central African Republic and southern Sudan to Kenya. From there it reaches all the way to South Africa where it is called the veldt.

In some areas there is 'sparse forest', in others only clumps of trees along the rivers with scattered thorn bushes elsewhere. In East Africa the savannah is split by the Great Rift valley. High rocky cliffs fall to the valley floor where ancient volcanoes interrupt the flat plain. Snow-capped mountains such as Mount Kilimanjaro in Tanzania and the rocky Mountains of the Moon on the borders of Uganda and Rwanda/Zaire tower over the surrounding countryside.

Most people think the savannah is dull and so it is. What impresses the traveller is its sheer size. Zimbabwe is larger than Britain or West Germany while Kenya is larger than France and Zaire's boundaries are as far apart as London is from the Caucasus. It is in the savannah that the traveller is awed by the vast spaces of Africa. The roads are dusty tracks, the towns small and far apart. Because of the dust and the road surfaces, you have to drive slowly, and at twenty-five miles an hour a giraffe can easily keep up with a car. Majestically he strides along, raising his proud neck above the bushes, looking down at you with benign wonder. Or there may be a herd of wildebeest, hundreds of them, or zebras, galloping through the tall grass. Even the huge elephant looks the right size in this immense landscape.

This is also the home of the lion, herds of antelope, reedbuck and gazelles, so graceful and quick that only the cheetah can outrun them.

Buffaloes wallow in the marshes and the hippopotamus shows only his nose, eyes and ears above the river water. Millions of birds flock to the rivers that cut through the savannah, their wide waters under wide skies, glittering in the dazzling sunlight. There are pelicans, storks, marabous, white herons, cormorants, ibis, crested cranes and many others. Eagles, kites and vultures soar in the skies, guinea fowl and ostrich run through the grass and there are always egrets and tick birds around the flocks of game. Song birds fill the space with sound, especially several species of turtle doves. Among the smaller animals are colourful chameleons, arm-long monitor lizards—and snakes—and everywhere there are insects.

All these living creatures may be characters in the African tales and the inventive storyteller will give each one its own personality: the lion is proud but lazy, the giraffe wise and silent, the jackal quick and cunning, the leopard angry and aggressive, the hyena greedy but stupid, the elephant friendly but clumsy. Every animal has its own human characteristics—for in the tales the animals are human beings in disguise.

We know that primitive man was born in Africa millions of years ago but we do not really know anything about the way in which the earliest people thought. We can only guess from the growth of languages in historical times and from some religions. The myths of Africa, passed down from long, long ago, give us an idea of an ancient view of reality.

Africans are very religious people. The early explorers did not realize this nor did the early missionaries, who described Africans as idolators and barbarians. Yet religion pervades every aspect of the life of an African. That does not mean that African societies are perfect, far from it. Life in Africa is hard and full of fears and suspicions.

It is not easy to discover the original African religions. In the southern lands, Christianity has become dominant while in the north, Islam is 'the only true faith'. It is in tropical Africa that the authentic African religions are still alive and functioning. The best known are those of the Yoruba in Nigeria and Ashanti in Ghana but there are hundreds of smaller religious groups. For these we have to search in old travellers' diaries and the accounts of early missionaries and patiently piece together fragments of oral tradition to obtain a coherent picture. Some of the most deeply held beliefs cannot be talked about, especially to strangers, and there are few well-structured accounts which correspond to the familiar myths and legends of Greece and Rome with their families of gods.

Most peoples in tropical and southern Africa accept the idea of a 'High God', or rather, a sky god who is often associated with thunder and lightning. The earth, the sun and the moon, are the most prominent gods; the seagods are worshipped among the western tribes. These are the good gods, although the sun sometimes has a double role: it causes life but also drought and so death. The earth is always a female deity who favours those who worship her but metes out inexorable punishment to the disobedient and neglectful.

The forest is a mysterious deity, elusive and whimsical. The forest contains almost everything its inhabitants need: fruits, game, wood for burning and making tools and furniture, bark for clothes, leaves for vegetables, lianas for rope and for snares, roots and juices for medicine and strong drink. Several central African peoples regard the forest as the abode of the gods, the other world where the spirits live, so that anyone wishing to enter it has to take special precautions and to perform certain rituals. It is also the abode of the *elokos*, who are dwarf-demons who devour human flesh and are masters of witchcraft. Finally, it is in the forest that the sorcerer will carve a piece of wood into which he will force a spirit to take up its abode. The spirit will then serve the sorcerer and travel to his master's enemies to kill them. This wooden statue is known as a fetish and is greatly feared and respected even today.

In the oldest versions of the myths, the characters are animals with awesome magic powers. The spider can climb up to heaven, the lion can devour a whole village full of people, the python reaches from horizon to horizon. Later, they become half man, half animal, characters who can be either evil demons or good spirits who help their human foster children. Gradually, several of the characters become almost entirely human, endowed with wisdom and helpfulness, as the animal world evolves into a pantheon of good gods and bad demons, still representing our own human characteristics and likely to resume animal shapes.

If these spiritual beings marry mortals they may have human children so that many clans claim descent from animal ancestors, who become their 'totems' or symbols.

The dividing line between gods and spirits is a very arbitrary one. Generally gods are more superhuman than spirits, they have more personality and show themselves more universally. Many African peoples believed that everything in nature had a spirit. Some spirits were strong and powerful like the strong-willed mind of a great chief or a killer lion. Some were weaker, more diffused, like the spirits of trees. Still, every tree had its own spirit and it could kill the man who chopped it down without performing the proper ceremony. This was necessary for the tree spirit would survive in the wood even after it had been made into a hut, a boat or a drum. Without the spirit's co-operation no good hut could be built, the boat would sink, the drum would remain silent.

The basic idea behind this is power. Everything we meet has a certain power. A lion, a snake, lightning and a river can kill people, so they must have very strong spirits. In English, too, we use the word 'spirit' in the sense of 'energy' and we know today that trees, animals, lightning and rivers do contain large amounts of energy which scientists see as a mechanical force—but which for many people is religious.

Africa has had great kingdoms, warriors and empires such as those of Benin, the Yoruba and the Ashanti and the mysterious civilizations of ancient Zimbabwe, Aksum and Meroe; but most communities were composed of a chief, his wives and their children. Gradually, retainers would cluster around the compound of the chief. These would be farmhands and builders. Later, skilled craftsmen might settle in the village, such as a blacksmith, boatbuilder and toolmaker who could cut shafts for spears and hoes. In the nomadic communities everything centres around the cattle, goats or camels. These have to be taken to the waterhole to drink, then to the pastures to graze and often to a salty place to lick the salt.

Many crafts are in the hands of women: plaiting mats and baskets, making pots and dishes, as well as collecting firewood and hoeing the fields. Girls have to fetch water, sometimes two hours walking away. Woodcarving, carpentry, hut building, cutting trees and weaving, are men's work.

Of course these are generalizations and there are many differences in various parts of Africa, where the peoples range from kings and chieftains who trace their descent back to the gods themselves, to forest pygmies, bushmen hunter-gatherers and nomadic cattle keepers. There are cities with old industries such as cloth dying and leatherwork, particularly in Nigeria. The arts of Africa are well known: wood sculpting, bronze and silver work and decorative painting, as well as music and dance.

The most important art in Africa is the art of language. Africa speaks more than a thousand languages. In some countries there is just one dominant language but in others there are many: Sudan, Cameroun and Nigeria each have over 200 distinct languages while Zaire, the largest African country, has over 325 languages from five distinct language groups. Even the 'small' nations of Ghana and Sierra Leone still speak twenty-two languages each.

The most important single language family are the Bantu languages (Bantu means 'people') spoken from Kenya to Cameroun and south to Namibia and South Africa.

There are also trading languages which are spoken by people from many different groups. The most important is Swahili, which has been used in the marketplace for so long that it is now spoken by millions as a second language. Also important is Hausa, which is spoken in northern Nigeria, Niger, northern Ghana and Chad; while Bambara, Dyula or Malinke is one of the most widespread languages reaching from Guinea and Liberia right across to Mali and Burkino Faso. Arabic is found all across North Africa and is often spoken in a simplified form. In Angola and Mozambique, Portuguese remains spoken by townspeople who have no other common tongue. English and French are commonly used in schools throughout Africa for religious or historical reasons.

In Africa there is a song for every type of work: there are hunting, hoeing, rowing, sailing, woodcutting, carrying, hutbuilding songs. There are also proverbs — over a thousand in every language. Both songs and proverbs form an integral part of African tales. Proverbs are still used in daily conversation to exercise social control or to express an opinion indirectly, without hurting anyone's feelings.

Among the greatest arts of all is the art of storytelling. In Africa there is electricity only in the cities. In the country it is dark after sunset at around six; few people have lamps and of course there is no television. What do they do? They tell stories. The good storyteller is still at a premium. He or she is an expert in many things, someone who has seen and heard amazing events, not someone who was born yesterday! The storyteller has his eyes and ears open, he knows people and disguises them as animals so that nobody's feelings are hurt. He knows the customs of the tribe and the importance of passing on traditional values and history. He knows the power of the spirits and the habits of the animals.

The stories in this book are just a small selection of the vast numbers of tales which express the fundamental beliefs of Africa. Africa is a different world or rather it is a thousand different worlds, some beautiful, some ugly but all interesting. Africa, the real Africa, is very different from anything you have ever seen.

In the beginning

From very earliest times, people everywhere have tried to understand the origins of the world they live in, the strange forces of nature around them and, above all, the origin of the human race itself. In Africa there are very many versions of the creation story, fitted to the circumstances and experience of the different peoples.

The Yoruba in Nigeria have a rich mythology, with gods and spirits who have great influence over the lives of human beings. Their story of creation is linked, like many others, to the origin of their own tribe.

Olodumare the god of the sky sent his two sons, Obatala and Oduduwa, down to this world with three things: a bag, a hen and a chameleon. At that time there was no land, only water, so the two brothers had nowhere to stand. Olodumare therefore dropped a tree from the sky, a coconut palm which grew so fast that it was already a high tree by the time Obatala and Oduduwa reached Earth. They landed safely in its branches.

Obatala at once started carving the bark of the tree to tap palm wine; he liked the taste so much that he stayed there and was soon fast asleep, for palm wine, formed from the sweet, fermented sap of the palm tree, is a powerful drink. Oduduwa, however, climbed down to the roots of the tree in the water. There he opened the bag they had brought and discovered that it contained white sand which he scattered on the surface of the water.

The chameleon they had brought came and walked on it very, very carefully, for such is the chameleon's character—and the sand held its weight. Then Oduduwa emptied the rest of the contents of the sack, a heap of rich black earth. The hen came and started scratching vigorously, scattering it in all directions until it spread out and became the land we know today.

When Oduduwa stepped on the land, his land, Olodumare sent Aje (prosperity) from heaven as a gift and she stayed with him there on earth for the rest of her life. Olodumare gave his son three other gifts: a bag of maize to sow for food; a bag of cowrie shells to trade with; and three iron bars which he forged into knives, machetes and hoes. So Oduduwa became the first king of Ife, the centre of the kingdom of Yorubaland.

The son of Oduduwa and Aje, who was named Oranyan, owned horses and became a great warrior who defended his nation against all attackers. They say that he never died but withdrew in old age to a cave in the rocks. Whenever his people are in danger, Oranyan will come again.

The Bakuba, a tribe from the damp rainforest regions of Zaire, have a kingdom with very ancient origins: their list of 122 kings is believed to stretch back in history to perhaps as early as the sixth century AD. In their myth of creation the universe was made by one god alone whose name was Mbombo.

In the beginning there was nothing but darkness and water which was ruled over by Mbombo, the great white spirit. One day he felt a terrible pain in his stomach and he vomited up the sun, moon and stars. Now there was light everywhere, and the fierce rays of the sun made the water turn to steam and rise up as clouds. Gradually, dry hills appeared as the level of the water dropped.

Mbombo vomited again, and this time trees came out of his mouth followed by animals, people and many other things: the first woman, the leopard, the eagle, the falling star, the anvil, the monkey Fumu, the first man, the firmament, the razor, medicine and lightning. Among all these there was only one troublemaker and that was lightning. It had such a fierce temper and caused so much trouble that eventually Mbombo chased it into the sky where it lives today. Mankind was now without fire since this had been provided by the lightning, so Mbombo showed the people how to draw fire out of the trees.
'There is fire in every tree,' he said, and he taught them how to make a tool known as a firedrill to obtain it. Sometimes though, the lightning still causes trouble when it leaps down and strikes the earth.

According to the same legend, the first woman had a son named Woto and a daughter named Labama. When Woto became a grown man, he moved westward with his children and changed their language by laying a medicine on their tongues. When they finally settled in the desert, Woto blew his horn and at once there arose out of the barren sand a whole forest of trees—a forest which still stands today near Salamudimu.

The Pangwe of Cameroun believe that God created first a lizard out of clay which he placed in a pool of water to soak. He left it there for seven days; at the end of this period God called, 'Man, come out,' and a man emerged instead of a lizard. This proves, say the Pangwe, that people once used to live in the water, in rivers and swamps.

Far away on the other side of the continent, the Shilluk, who live along the Nile in the Sudan, also tell how Juok (their name for the high god) created men out of clay. They relate how Juok travelled north and found some white clay out of which he fashioned Europeans; the Arabs were made out of reddish brown clay; the Africans from black earth.

Juok said to himself, 'I will give men long legs to run in the shallows while fishing, like the pink flamingoes; I will give them long arms to swing a hoe the way monkeys swing sticks; I will give them mouths to eat millet and tongues to sing with; and I will give them eyes to see their food and ears to hear their songs.'

The Nubians in northern Sudan have a slightly different explanation for the races of Man. They say that God made a man of clay and then baked him in his bread oven. Anxious to have his man well done, God left him too long in the oven, so when he came out, he was a black man. God sent him up the Nile to the land of the burned-faces: Ethiopia. God then made another clay-man and put him in the oven. Afraid he might be burned too, God took him out too early so he was a white man. God sent him downstream to live in the northern countries. Finally, the third clay man was taken out at the right time and he was nicely 'terra cotta' coloured, reddish brown. He was allowed to stay there on the Nile in Sudan where God created Man.

The Yao who live on the eastern shores of Lake Malawi believe that people first came from the water. It was because of them that God, Mulungu, was driven away to heaven.

At first there were no people in the world, only Mulungu and the animals, and as a result life was peaceful and cruelty was unknown. Then one day the chameleon decided to make a fishtrap which he dropped into the river. On the first day it was filled with fish which the chameleon ate heartily, but the next morning there was nothing in it and the morning after that, all it contained was a tiny man and woman.

The chameleon had never seen anything like them before and he took them to Mulungu to ask what they were.

'Release them from your trap and let them walk on the ground,' Mulungu said after studying them closely. 'They will soon grow.'

The chameleon did as he was asked and the tiny couple quickly grew as tall as people are today. All the animals watched them curiously to see what they would do. The very first thing they did was to rub two sticks together to make fire. From a tiny spark, the fire soon grew out of control and blazed through the forest so that the animals had to run for their lives.

The man and woman caught and killed a buffalo which they roasted in the flames, and each day after that they made another fire and killed another animal to cook and eat.

'They are burning everything,' Mulungu cried in anguish. 'They are killing my people!'

All the animals ran into the forest to get as far from the man and woman as they could. The chameleon ran up the trunk of a tall tree and climbed high in its branches. The spider climbed so high that he disappeared into the sky. Even Mulungu ran from the man and the woman.

'How did you climb into the sky?' called Mulungu.

'With this,' shouted the spider and he spun out a rope which he lowered down to Mulungu. Mulungu climbed up it and went to live in the sky, where he has lived ever since. And that is how Mulungu was driven from the earth by the wickedness of mankind.

The lizard and the chameleon

The Zulus live mainly in Zululand, Natal in South Africa. In the nineteenth century they were a formidable fighting force but in 1879 they were defeated by the British and their military power came to an end. They once had an elaborate cosmology—their own interpretation of the world—but although they have a strong tradition of folk stories, most of their ancient myths have been forgotten. This creation story was recorded by Dr Wilhelm Bleek, librarian at Cape Town, during his research tour in Zululand in 1855-56.

In the beginning there was a large swamp in the lands to the north, called Uhlanga. Here grew many types of reeds and rushes, each with its own colour.

One morning the sky-god descended from heaven and married Uhlanga. Out of this vast valley he broke off many reeds of different colours and made them into people. He made them in pairs, a man and a woman from every type of reed. These original people were called Ukulunkulu, or Ancestor.

Then the Great One placed the Sun and Moon in the sky, saying 'Let the sun travel by day and the moon travel by night.'

He brought forth the Bantu people and the white people, as well as cattle, sheep, goats and dogs. He created all the animals of the wilderness, all the birds and insects of the veldt and forest; and all of the fish and the other creatures of the rivers and lakes.

One day the Great One called to Unwaba the chameleon and said, 'Go to the people I have made and tell them, "People shall not die."'

The chameleon set out on its way down to earth, treading slowly and carefully along the branches. It took a very long time and before it had reached its destination, the Great One had changed his mind. He summoned Intulo the lizard, saying, 'Go to the people and say that all of them will die eventually. The cattle, the sheep, the dogs—everything that lives will die. Nothing will remain on earth for ever.'

All this time Unwaba the chameleon was treading steadily onward, stopping occasionally to nibble the leaves of the shrubs, then reaching out one cautious leg after the other. Intulo ran fast, scurrying along to carry out the Great One's command. Intulo arrived first on Earth and, obeying the Great One, proclaimed his message:
'All the people will die, both white and black. All the animals will die, both tame and wild. Nothing will remain.'

Soon afterwards, the chameleon also arrived and after looking carefully around, called the people to listen to its message. It was too late. The word of the Great One cannot be taken back; the message of Intulo the lizard, bringing death to the world, remained. And from that time on, all living things have been doomed to die and to leave their children behind.

It is said that when the Great One created the human race, he created not just the white and the black but all the nations of men and animals: the Sun people, the Elephant people, the Bushmen and many, many more. From the Bantu he created thirty-one separate tribes. When he had finished making the living things, the Great One looked at the land and spoke. 'Let water come forth so that the people and animals I have made may drink from it. Let fire come forth so that people can cook their food. Here is the earth, red and fertile. Let the women dig it. Here are the trees. Let the men cut them to build their houses. Let the men make hoes and give them to the women so that they can plant seeds and grow millet. The women must fetch firewood from the forest and grind the corn and cook the food. The men will guard the cattle and fight to keep the people safe.

'A woman shall be given by her father in exchange for cattle. If a man knows how to care for his people he will know how to care for his cattle so that his sons will inherit the shining beasts after he has grown old and died.'

The original Zulu myth, passed down from generation to generation by the storytellers of the tribe, contained the rules by which the people lived, emphasizing the importance of the cattle which gave them food, milk and by which they measured their wealth. Many of their sacred beliefs have never been explained to a stranger and much of the old tradition has been lost as their way of life has changed.

Variations of the chameleon story are told in many parts of Africa; sometimes he is overtaken by a hare, sometimes by a snake, but always the result is the same. The message of life arrives too late—and mankind is doomed to die.

The Swahili story of creation

Arab traders first visited East Africa in the eighth century AD, dealing mainly in ivory and slaves. Their influence over the continent has been very great and today almost 200 million Africans follow the religion of Islam. This story of the creation of the world is the African version of ancient Semitic beliefs that have influenced the Bible and the Koran.

In the beginning there was only God, century after century. When he decided to create the light, that was the first morning: light spread to the horizons of the night sky in all the colours of the rainbow and the Lord was pleased with its beauty. Out of this light He created the souls of all the human beings who would live in the future, for God already knew all the things that had not yet come to be. The souls of the prophets were created first, then the souls of the saints and holy people, the pious and devout worshippers who would live only for him. Their souls shine in the darkness for ever. After these, the Lord created the myriads of souls of ordinary people which shine like the stardust in the sky. The angels, too, were created out of light so clear that they can never lie, because their luminous bodies are transparent so that they contain only purity and the desire to worship God and help people.

After the light, God created seven great things: the Canopy, the Throne, the Pen, the Book, the Trumpet, Paradise and Hellfire.

Firstly, the Canopy is like a tent or pavilion above the immense and immutable Throne upon which the Lord resides and which was the second object that he made.

Thirdly, God created the Pen which reaches from sky to earth and writes the fate and destiny of all men and women day and night.

Fourthly, there was the Book: the record in which all events that will ever take place are written down for all the centuries to come so that whatever misfortune happens, the pious man will not rebel against God but instead exclaim, 'It is written, it is His will!'

Fifthly, the Trumpet of the Last Day will announce the end of the world and God's final judgement over all the souls He created.

The sixth thing that God created was Paradise, the garden of delight where the good and obedient souls will live in eternal bliss, loving God and each other.

The seventh thing that God made was the great fire of Hell where the wicked will live in eternal torture.

Beneath his throne, God created a gigantic tree called the Cedar of the End. On this tree there are millions of leaves, some fresh and green, others old and withering: these are our lives. God has written a name on each leaf, because He knows every one of us by name. When He wills, a leaf comes whirling down, but before it reaches the earth an angel arrives, reads the name on the leaf and tells the angel of death. The angel of death, who is called in Swahili Nduli Mtwaa-roho or 'the taker of souls', will descend immediately to earth, find the owner of that name wherever he or she is hiding and announce, 'Your hour has come, your time is past.' Death will then part body and soul forthwith, for death gives no delay.

After this God created the earth and the sun which rises above it. The earth was one vast

ocean and the warm rays of the sun made the mists rise up to form colourful clouds which travel from one end of the sky to the other. Then God commanded the land to rise out of the ocean; surveying the barren lands, God created green vegetation. Forests of tall trees rose to cover the steep sides of the mountains; waves of plumed grasses decorated the hills, rows of whispering palm trees nodded along the seashore.

Then God made the sun decline in the west, painted the skies red and gold and took the light out of the world. He suspended numerous bright lights in the sky which He called stars and caused each of them to move along a path that He had assigned to it. Only He knows how many stars there are and where they go. For God everything is easy, since the unfathomed sky is far beneath His presence.

Next, God created an enormous cockerel with many-coloured feathers that stands in Heaven and crows every morning just before dawn so that the cockerels on earth can hear him. They, too, then begin to crow so that the people will know that it is time to rise and worship the Lord. There is no more important work on earth or in Heaven. After the cockerel crowed for the first time, the sun rose and the day began on the earth, which resembled a flat pancake floating on a wide ocean.

Now, God created the animals in four classes: those that swim, whose king is the whale; those that creep, whose king is the python; those that fly, whose king is the eagle; and those that walk on four legs, whose king is the lion. Likewise there are four classes of creatures gifted with intelligence: the angels made out of the light; the jinns or wind spirits made from air; the satans or evil spirits made from fire; and finally human beings made from earth. All God's creatures are born and so they all must eventually die because nothing will live for ever except for God.

The flat earth and the ocean surrounding it is like a filled saucer which God placed on the four horns of a bull (some say that it is a cow, but only God knows). This animal stands on the back of a huge fish which swims in another ocean, the depth of which is unknown. The earth is composed of seven layers with air between them, like the floors of a tower. The first earth (the top floor) is inhabited by humans, the children of Adam.

The second floor, one floor down, is the abode of the winds. The winds live immediately underneath the earth, and that is why caves are such draughty places: the winds are constantly coming and going through them into our world.

On the third earth there live a race of people with dog faces and big ears. They are better than the children of Adam because they never rebelled against the Lord so they will not be punished on the day of judgement. They are really disguised angels.

The fourth earth is where the guardian of the fire stores his mountains of sulphur and brimstone to feed his many fires.

On the fifth floor there lives a race of scorpions that are as big as camels and which have tails like steel chains. Each tail contains a ton of poison, one drop of which would kill all of the fishes in the ocean.

On the sixth floor are the souls of the doomed who are being beaten with red hot steel staves until the end of eternity.

The seventh floor is the deepest part of the underworld and there lives Iblis, the Devil. He resides on his throne surrounded by demons whom he sends out to spy on the children of Adam and tempt them into error. However, the real Hell lies even deeper below in the deepest part of the universe. It was created out of God's wrath, and those who live in it would have to climb for seventy years before they emerged from this abyss. Hell, too, is constructed in seven levels and in the very lowest the souls of the worst criminals shiver in eternal cold.

Stories of the sun and moon

Many African peoples have myths which explain the origin of the sun, moon and stars. The Bushmen, for example, believe that the sun once lived on earth. His light shone out only when he lifted his arm and then only lit a small area around his hut. Some children, however, managed to creep up to him while he was asleep and threw him bodily up into the sky so that his light filled the whole world. It is the Bushmen of the Kalahari, too, who say that the Milky Way was formed when a girl threw a handful of wood ash up into the sky; she also formed the individual stars that shine so brightly in the clear air of the desert from fragments of red and yellow roots. The Yoruba of Nigeria say the sun was made by Obatala, son of the sky god. It happened like this.

There was once a king of the forest who had a lovely Iroko tree, but because he forgot to sacrifice to the gods the tree fell down and would have crushed his house completely if Obatala had not intervened. Before the branches even touched the roof, Obatala had magically turned the tree into the secret precious metal known as gold. Then Obatala summoned the blacksmith of heaven and told him to make a jar and a boat from the precious metal. Once these were made, he ordered his slave, whose name was Youdonthearwhatisay, to take the golden jar and sail in the golden boat

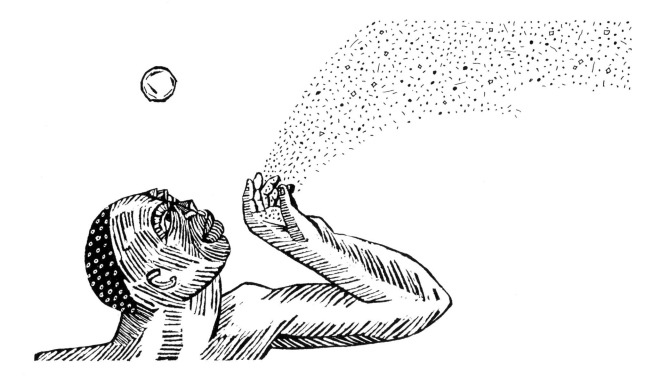

up to the top of the sky and then down again on the other side. And so the sun began its first journey.

Oludumare, the sky god, created the moon in the shape of a flintstone with a thin side and a round side. He placed it in the sky and there it slowly spins around, showing us its full round side only for three nights of the month.

Other stories, like this one told by the Wute of Cameroun, explain why the sun is brighter than the moon.

In the earliest days of the world, the sun and the moon shone with equal radiance in the sky, the sun by day and the moon by night. They were good friends and often went out together until one day the sun suggested they both take a bath in the river, each with his own family. The moon agreed and the sun proposed that he go and bathe upstream around a bend. This was also agreed for in Africa decency and decorum are always maintained.

The sun said, 'I shall go in first. When you see the water seething and boiling you will know that I have entered the water.' With these words he walked away with his family. When they were well out of sight of the moon and his children, the sun ordered his own children to

cut dry branches, set fire to them and throw them into the river. As soon as the moon saw the water steaming and boiling, he thought the sun had taken his bath and he, too, went into the water. Enormous clouds of steam billowed up and the river boiled for miles downstream.

Alas! When the moon came out of this bath he was quite pale and had lost all his heat and much of his brilliance. So when the sun reappeared he mocked his friend, 'Now I shine the brighter of us two.'

The moon perceived that the sun had been jealous and had never had any intention of bathing in the river. He decided to take a bloody revenge for this trickery. Some time later a terrible famine took place and many people died. The moon went to the sun and suggested they kill all their children and wives. 'I will go upstream with my people, and when you see blood in the river you will know that I have disposed of my entire family. In this time of famine we can no longer afford to keep so many people.' The sun agreed and as soon as he saw red water flowing downstream he killed all his wives and children and threw their bodies in the river.

The moon, however, had never had any

intention of killing his family. He had simply ordered his boys to throw red clay into the river so that the water was stained completely red. So there was the sun all alone and there he still is, shining brightly every day whereas the moon can be seen at night, pale and cool but surrounded by his wives and many, many little children. The moral that the Wute find in this story is that you cannot trust even your daily companions.

Once a man from the Kamba tribe of Kenya decided that he wanted to see the place where the sun rises every morning. He took some food for the journey and travelled east until he came to a wide river. He swam for a long time, frightened by the thought of crocodiles and finally reached the other bank and travelled further. His food had long since been finished, so he had to eat earth. At last he came to a second river, even wider than the first. The other side seemed to be on fire.
'This river is too large,' he thought, 'I can never cross it. But he closed his eyes, plunged into the water and was carried to the other side by the current. There he met an old woman.
'Where does the sun live?' he asked her.
'Up on that hill,' she said, so the man climbed the hill and saw a palace made from light. Everything was made of gold! He was taken to the sun's wife who received him kindly and gave him food and cool water to drink. After a time he saw something red coming nearer and nearer. It was the sun himself, home from a day's work in the sky. The sun greeted his guest courteously and invited him to stay for supper and to spend the night. Then he showed his guest round his palace, a magnificent building with arches made of cloud-pearls.

The next morning the man was up at first light so that he could see the sun rise. He actually saw the bed from which the sun rose to begin the day. They had soup for breakfast and the sun's wife gave the man some bread for his family. Then the sun said, 'Close your eyes,' and when the man opened them again, he was standing outside his own hut and his own family were just coming out to start their daily work. Together, they ate the sun-bread and from that time on, they were never ill again.

The finding of fire

Long, long ago people did not know fire. They never cooked anything, they could not forge iron or bake pots and they had to eat raw meat. Once there was a hunter who had strayed far from his home while pursuing a beautiful big bird whose bright colours had attracted him. Finally, he lost sight of it and was just wondering whether to go home empty-handed or to continue his search, when he saw something he had never seen before: a thin cloud rising straight up into the air. Wondering what it could be, the hunter turned and went in the direction of what we know as smoke.

It took him much longer than he had expected to reach it, for a cloud of smoke may hang high in the air and be visible at a great distance. The sun set and night fell so that the hunter could no longer see the cloud, but just as he was about to turn back, he saw a light on the horizon. Now people who have no fire cannot have a light at night, for how would they light a lamp or a candle without fire? The man had never seen a light, except a star, and stars cannot be seen below the horizon. So he went in the direction of this new phenomenon to find out what was causing it.

When he came closer, he saw that the light changed its brilliance just like a star, but that unlike a star it had tongues shooting up from it, and sent out a swirling cloud. It was so full of movement and so hot when he came close to it, that the hunter decided it must be a powerful spirit. After a lot of hesitation and careful observation he approached the fire and addressed it, 'Great chief, I greet you! The sun has set. How are you?'

The fire answered these polite phrases with its crackling voice, 'Welcome, man, you may stay the night with me and warm yourself. But you must feed me trees and shrubs, trunks and dead branches, dry grass and reeds!'

Astonished, the hunter went out and collected dead branches and sticks, which he threw on the fire one by one, as the fire instructed him. He saw to his immense surprise how the fire grew rapidly to gigantic proportions as he put a big branch on it.

'If you want food too, man, look behind you.' The man did and saw a hare sitting there gazing into the fire, hypnotized by its light. Quickly he drew an arrow and shot it. He was about to eat it raw, as was his custom, when the fire spoke to him, 'Come here man, and roast your food so that you may like it better.'

The man had never heard the word 'roast', so he did not know how to go about it. He soon found that the best way was to fix the meat on his spearblade. When he ate the roasted meat he decided that he would never again eat raw meat. He also decided, while he was eating, that he wanted to take the fire home with him so he could have light, warmth and roast meat every night. He proposed this to the fire, promising it that he would feed it well and look after it for as long as he lived. However, the fire declined politely, but firmly.
'I must never be allowed to travel, that would be dangerous for you and for all other living beings. I will stay here where God created me, do not ever try to take me away. You may come here as often as you like to warm yourself, to feed me and to roast your meat, but never tell anyone about me for they might come and steal me.'

The man promised and that night he slept warmly near the fire. The next morning he rose, well rested and said, 'Goodbye to you, fire, thank you, I will be back.'

When he arrived home he gave his wife some of the roasted meat he had brought, but he should never have done that, because she continually asked him for more. The man returned to visit the fire more and more often to warm himself and roast meat. Gradually he learned how to keep the fire burning nicely with big logs and how to revive it with dry leaves when he had been away too long and he found it smouldering in its ashes.

Of course, his wife told a friend about her husband's long absences and the delicious meat he brought home, and the friend decided to follow the hunter one day. He walked behind the hunter at a safe distance until he saw the smoke, and then the fire. He crept up closer as darkness fell and he saw the hunter place branches on the fire. When the hunter went to

sleep the friend saw his opportunity: he came near very quietly, grabbed a branch that was sticking out from under the fire, and ran away with it, leaving behind a trail of sparks.

As he ran, the fire went on eating the branch until it burned his hand. He dropped it, crying with pain and ran on. He had not gone far when he heard a roaring behind him. Turning, he saw the fire following him, many times larger than before, with threatening flames. He screamed and fled.

As it ran along the savannah, the fire devoured the grass on all sides, then the shrubs, then whole trees. It seemed to grow and divide itself into several streams of fire, each moving with the wind across the savannah until it reached from horizon to horizon. It seemed that the whole sky was going to catch fire and that the stars would soon be ablaze. Although the fire thief ran and ran, the fire easily caught up with him and encircled him, so that he could go no further. As the fire roared past, however, he discovered how he could keep out of its way for it never burned the same place twice: it would not return to a plot of grass or wood it had already eaten.

The fire spread on until it was finally stopped by a river but not before it had eaten up all the villages in its path. The villagers saved their lives by wading across the river. When the fire had finally burned itself out they returned cautiously to the ruins of their huts. There they found their food had been burned but as they were very hungry they tried to eat what was left of it. To their surprise they discovered that if it was not actually scorched black, it tasted much better than the uncooked food they were used to. They also discovered that their clay pots had not been eaten by the fire but had been hardened, 'baked' as we now call the process. Ever since then, people have been 'firing' their earthenware to make it more usable.

What had happened to the first fire while all this was going on? As soon as the hunter heard the new fire roaring in the surrounding woods, he woke up and was greatly surprised. The original fire was still there, quietly burning the wood he had fed it. It began to speak.
'A man came and tried to steal me. Now you

can see what happens when I leave this rocky place. My work is the destruction of nature. But I can also help you to make things: I can fire your pots for you and cook your food in them. I will bake your porridge so that you will have pancakes. I will melt iron for you so that you can make weapons and kill more food. And from the iron you will one day make the fire-wagon which I will drive with my steam so that it will pull your trains through the whole country.'

From that day onward, fire has stayed with us, and remains a valued friend — when it is treated with respect.

Kings and kingdoms

There have been many great kingdoms in Africa of which Egypt is one of the earliest and most famous. Two other ancient kingdoms were Napata (in what is now the Sudan) in the tenth century BC and Meroe which existed on the Nile from 670 BC onward. West Africa also had many important kingdoms: the empire of Ghana was founded in AD 700 and by 1067 an Arab explorer could write, 'The king of Ghana can put 200,000 warriors in the field ... he sits in a pavilion around which stand ten pages holding shields and gold-mounted swords.' By comparison a year earlier William I could assemble only 7000 men with which to conquer England. In 1235 Sundiata became king of Mali, founding the Keita dynasty which lasted for two centuries. Christian kings ruled in Nubia for almost a thousand years until the sixteenth century, while on the east coast Pate (in Kenya) and Kilwa (in Tanzania) were ruled by Islamic sultans in the Middle Ages.

The massive stone ruins of Zimbabwe are the remains of what was probably a royal palace and shrine, and were constructed by Bantu peoples between the eleventh and nineteenth centuries AD. At its most powerful, this kingdom controlled much of the territory between the Zambezi and Limpopo rivers. One of the best known of recent African kingdoms was that of the Zulus in southern Africa. They were once small and disunited tribes but at the beginning of the nineteenth century they were conquered and united by a chief named Chaka who welded them into a formidable fighting machine which conquered much of the surrounding territory. Their later kings Dingana and Cetawayo strongly resisted the advancing European settlers but in 1879 their military power was finally ended when they were defeated by the British.

These are only some of the many kingdoms founded in Africa. Their organizations differed greatly. Christian monarchs ruled 'by the grace of God'; Islamic rulers vowed to uphold the law of the Koran; in some nations a king's son succeeded his father and the dead man became an ancestral spirit worshipped by the whole nation.

The kingdom of Buganda lies near the equator in the fertile area around Lake Victoria in what is now Uganda. Its kings trace their descent from a man named Kintu who invaded the area from the north, establishing a powerful monarchy there. This Kintu may have been a historical character but the stories told for generations about him have become combined with ancient myths of creation enabling his descendants to trace their origins to the gods themselves.

When Kintu first came to Uganda he found that there was no food at all in the country; he had brought one cow with him and for some time he lived entirely on the milk she gave him. One day, however, the sons of Gulu (which means Sky) and their sister Nambi came down to the Earth and saw him.

They talked for a while and Nambi was impressed by Kintu's character. 'Kintu is good, I like him. Let me marry him,' she said.
'Sister,' they cautioned. 'You do not even know if this is a human being.'
'Does an animal build a house?' she asked, pointing to Kintu's grass hut.

However, she agreed to return to consult their father, Gulu. The brothers explained to him privately that they were suspicious of Kintu.
'He does not eat ordinary food,' they said. 'How can our sister marry him?'
'Let us steal the cow,' said Gulu, 'and see whether he dies or not.'

That night they crept down and carried Kintu's cow away with them. Of course Kintu was at a loss what to eat for he had had nothing but milk before, but he managed to find leaves, fruits and roots and somehow he survived.

Nambi had not been told of her father's test but she guessed when she saw the cow, and complaining that her brothers wished to kill the man she loved, she went down to earth to see what had happened to him.
'Come back with me,' she said. 'I know where your cow is, come and take it back.'

Kintu went with her to Heaven. There he was astounded to see many people, with well-made houses, rich herds of cattle, goats and sheep and chickens running about among groves of plantain trees. He had never seen such things before.

When Nambi's brothers saw Kintu sitting

with their sister at her house, they told Gulu and he ordered them to arrange another test. An enormous meal, enough for more than a hundred people, was cooked in Kintu's honour and he was shut inside a hut alone to consume it. 'If you do not eat it,' said Gulu, 'you are not Kintu. You shall not have the cow and you shall not have my daughter.'

Kintu ate and drank as much as he could, but a huge pile of food still remained and he was ready to despair when he saw that a great hole had appeared in the floor of the house. He immediately tipped all the beer and food into it and the hole closed up to hide it.
'Come and take away the empty baskets,' he called and although the brothers searched every corner of the house they could find no trace of any food: amazingly, it seemed that Kintu had eaten it all.

Once more, Gulu decided to test the stranger and this time he gave Kintu a copper axe and said, 'I need some kindling for my fire. Go and cut me some rocks: ordinary firewood is no use.'
'What am I to do?' said Kintu to himself. 'If I strike rock with the axe it will either break its edge or rebound and cut me.' However, when he examined the rocks he found they were cracked in places and he was able to prise off several pieces and bring them back to Gulu.

Still the King of Heaven was not satisfied and he devised yet another impossible task.
'Go and fill this pot with water,' ordered Gulu, 'but bring me dew only. I do not drink water from wells.'

Kintu was baffled but he refused to show it and, taking a water-pot, set out for the open grassland. He sat all night wondering how he could collect enough dew to satisfy Gulu, but in the early morning the thick blades of grass all around him were covered in heavy dew and the water pot itself was full to the brim.

At last Gulu was convinced that Kintu was a man fit to marry his daughter.
'This man is a wonderful being,' he told his people. 'He shall marry my daughter. But first he must pick out his cow from among my royal herd.'

Kintu knew that Gulu's herd was immense:

there were thousands of cattle, all looking just like his own cow. While he was wondering what to do a large bee flew up and settled on his shoulder.

'Take the one upon whose horns I settle,' it buzzed. 'That will be your cow.'

The next morning Kintu went to the appointed place and found the bee resting in a tree nearby. A large herd of cows was driven towards him and he pretended to look for his own among them. In fact he was watching the bee carefully: it did not move.

'My cow is not there,' said Kintu after a time.

A second herd was brought; again the bee did not move and again Kintu said, 'My cow is not there.'

Then they brought an even larger herd and this time the bee flew straight to one of the largest cows and rested on her back.

'That is my cow,' said Kintu firmly, striking her with his stick. The bee flew to a young heifer. 'And that is one of the calves she has born here.' The bee flew to a second heifer, then to a third, and each one Kintu claimed for his own.

Gulu was delighted with Kintu's success. 'You are truly Kintu,' he said. 'Take your cows; no-one can deceive you, you are too clever for that. Take my daughter, too, and go back with her to your home.'

So Kintu and Nambi were married and Gulu sent them down to live on earth, giving them a goat, a sheep, a chicken, a plantain-tree and seeds for all the edible tubers and leaves they needed.

'Hurry, now,' he told them, 'for you must leave before your brother Walumbe (which means Death) returns. He will want to go with you. And be sure not to return if you find you have forgotten anything, for Walumbe will follow you and you must go without him.'

On the way, Nambi remembered that she had forgotten to bring grain for the chicken and insisted on returning to fetch it. 'Don't worry,' she told Kintu, 'I will hurry back and no-one will see me.'

As she was collecting the grain from the doorway where she had left it, Gulu found her. 'Did I not tell you must not return if you forgot something?' he said. 'Now your brother

Walumbe will see you and he will go with you.'

Nambi tried to steal away secretly but Walumbe was too quick for her and together they returned to the place where Kintu was waiting. So Nambi, Kintu and Walumbe returned to earth together. Nambi planted her garden with the plantain-tree and the seeds and roots they had brought from the sky kingdom; and she and Kintu lived happily for they had children and there was food of all kinds for the family to eat. For a time Walumbe did not trouble them but Death cannot be avoided forever and eventually he took first one child, then another from them. Since then, in spite of all their efforts, Death has killed people whenever he could; but Kintu's family was not defeated. His children grew and prospered, founding a line of kings whose descendants, they say, are living to this day.

The Golden Stool

In some regions of West Africa men have personal stools, low wooden seats which are often expensively decorated. It is believed that a part of a man's spirit lives in his stool and some men even carry it around with them so that no-one can steal it; that would mean loss of face as well as loss of spirit. A man who brings his own stool with him to a meeting is saved the embarrassment of looking for a place to sit in the circle of councillors, especially if he arrives there uninvited. No-one may sit on a man's personal stool except his oldest son, after his death. For a king the stool represents his authority over the land, just as the British refer to 'the Throne' meaning the sovereign.

The greatest of all the royal stools of West Africa belongs to the Kings of Ashanti, the nation of the Akan-speaking people who live in what is now Ghana. More than two hundred years ago, before the Ashanti became one nation they were divided into feuding tribes, each with its own leader. Osai Tutu was king of one of them. One day in 1697 there appeared at his court a famous medicine man called Anotchi. He told the king that it had pleased

God to give Osai Tutu sovereignty over all the Ashanti. Anotchi persuaded the king to convene a grand council of all the clan chiefs at which he would perform a ceremony that would confirm Osai Tutu as sovereign.

The chiefs assembled and Anotchi called upon Nyame (God) to demonstrate by a sign that he confirmed Osai Tutu as king. All eyes were fixed on heaven, and there descended from the sky a stool made of pure gold. Majestically it placed itself before the king as if inviting him to take possession of it. Anotchi told the king and the assembled dignitaries that this Golden Stool contained the soul of the Ashanti nation and that their health and welfare were in it. The stool symbolized the unity of the nation and no-one was ever allowed to sit on it. Even the king and his successors used it only ceremonially during the rite of enthronement, but never to sit on. All the assembled chiefs and dignitaries were persuaded by this miracle to recognize Osai Tutu as the paramount ruler of all the Ashanti.

The Ashanti kings overcame all their enemies in the following decades but in 1872 a war broke out with the British and finally, fearing that continued fighting would endanger the Golden Stool, the Ashanti offered their surrender. The British commander who arrived in Kumasi to accept their surrender demanded to sit on the Golden Stool, imagining it to be simply the throne of the kingdom of Ashanti, and hoping in that way ceremonially to subdue the nation. The opposite happened. A new war broke out in 1896 in which the Ashanti appeared to be ready to fight to the death. The European invaders did not understand that the Golden Stool was not the king's seat but that the life and spirit of the nation itself resided in it. Before the British occupied the capital city of Kumasi, the king's senior ministers buried the Golden Stool in a secret place.

Twenty-five years later, in 1921, some workmen were digging a ditch for a new road when they found a hoard of golden ornaments. They were searching for more when a very old man appeared and told them that if they dug another spadeful they would all die of smallpox. By chance they had stumbled on the hiding place of the Golden Stool. The frightened workmen ran away and refused to return to work. That night, the old man had the stool dug up by his own trusted servants and removed to another secret place. However, some of the priceless ornaments buried it were stolen and later offered for sale. A new rebellion threatened when this was discovered and the thieves had to be put in prison to save their lives. This time, however, the British authorities acted with more sagacity and permitted the Golden Stool to be returned to its rightful place in the palace at Kumasi where it still is today.

The moonprince

Long, long ago, before any other king had ruled the Basotho people there arrived a king who had the moon on his chest. This large, brilliant disc was so bright that when the king walked around at night the people could see each other and do their work. They called him Khoedi-Sefubeng which means 'Moon-in-Chest'. Nobody disputed his right to reign when he arrived and he governed the country for many years. He had ten wives which should not surprise us since he was probably a god. Do earthly creatures give light in the dark?

One day the king, who possessed knowledge of the future, announced that each of his wives would give him a son, but that only one of his ten sons would be created after his image, with a full moon on his chest. The other boys would only have stars and crescents to show, but of course they would still be beautifully luminous and be far superior to other children born of normal human fathers. Soon it became apparent that the king had spoken truly and that all his wives were happily expecting. When their time was fulfilled they all gave birth to sons, and every baby boy had a bright star or a crescent moon shining on his little chest. But only one had a full moon, which filled the hut of his mother with soft milky light.

His mother lay sleeping deeply with the baby beside her. She was Morongoe, the king's favourite wife. Naturally, the other wives were envious of her, but who can change destiny? One of the wives was furious with jealousy when she saw the silvery light shining out into the night. She bribed the old midwife and told her, 'That little boy with his moon must be disposed of. Hide him in a corner and put this puppy in his place.'

The old woman obeyed and the baby moonprince was laid in a corner of his mother's hut behind piles of old sleeping mats, pots, jars and other clutter. A newly born puppy of one of the king's hunting hounds was put in his place beside his mother and when she woke up she was told, 'You have given birth to a dog.' She cried long and sadly, but history does not relate whether Morongoe believed such an extraordinary lie.

When the king was told by his second wife that Morongoe had given birth to a young dog, he decided to divorce her and give her as a maid to his second wife. The jealous wife, of course, expected that the moonprince would die; only then would she be happy for then her own baby son, who had only a half moon on his breast, would become crown prince. But who can change the course of destiny? The moonprince did not die, he was fed by the mice who lived in the king's compound and had plenty of food. They brought the baby prince crumbs soaked in milk, and heaps of mafi, a type of yoghurt, and so he not only survived, he thrived.

Weeks later, the king's second wife—and now his favourite—was walking proudly through the compound early one night when she saw a bright ray of moonlight that did not descend from the sky, it slanted upwards out of Morongoe's door. The queen was furious—and also frightened—for she knew it signified that the moonprince had not died. So she went up to the king and said, 'Your majesty, Morongoe is still living in her old queen's hut. Don't you think it is time to have that hut burned? It is full of old rubbish and mice and other vermin, I should like to see the whole place cleaned up.' The next morning the king ordered his men to burn Morongoe's hut to the ground. Fortunately, a mouse was sitting under the king's throne just at that time and he immediately scurried off to tell the others what was happening. That night the mice took the old sleeping mat on which the moonprince was sleeping, and dragged it out of the hut. I do not know how many mice helped in pulling, there may have been hundreds of them. They went with him all the way to the old cattle kraal and approached a cow whose calf had been slaughtered to celebrate the birth of the prince with the half-moon.

The mice said to the old cow, 'We bring you the heir to the throne. He has been with us since he was born but now one of us who was sitting under the throne, heard the queen say that she wants the hut burned to the ground. She wants him killed of course, that is why we

bring him to you to nurse him.' Consequently, the motherly cow accepted the moonprince and fed him.

The next day Morongoe's hut was burned so that many of the mice who lived there perished. Queen Morongoe had to go and live with the maids.

Months later, on a dark, moonless night, the second queen was again walking around in the king's compound when her attention was drawn by a faint light that looked like moonshine. On a moonless night? The queen approached the place from which the light was coming. It was the old cowshed and she had no doubt that she would find the moonprince there. She found him by the light of the little moon on his own breast. He was sucking the old cow's milk which was still plentiful. How big he was! He must have grown more than the other children who were born the same night but who had only stars and crescent moons on their chests. And there it was, the full moon on the boy's breast, growing with its owner, for he was no longer a baby, that was clear!

She hurried to see the king and when she saw he was in a favourable mood, she flattered him with honey-sweet words, then said coaxingly, 'Your majesty's court would look much better if there were not this old cattle kraal still in it. You now have so many cattle you should build a new kraal for them outside the town. Why

don't you have the old kraal burned down and slaughter the old cow? She is much too old for anything now.'

The king promised to do as she asked him, but do you know what happened in the meantime? The spy-mouse who had his hiding place right under the king's throne, ran quickly to the old cow and told her exactly what the king had discussed with his queen.

'Take the young moonprince and carry him to safety,' he ended. 'Take him to the lake in the valley and give him to the crabs, they will look after him, I'm sure.'

The cow was alarmed at the prospect that her kraal, where she had lived all her life, would be burned down. She told the little prince, who could already stand up and walk, to climb on her neck and hold her horns for they were going on a journey. Then she walked away with him, the moon on his chest lighting the path as they went.

She walked out of the village towards the lake, down to the valley where the crabs lived, and told them the story of the poor prince who was persecuted by his own step-mother. The crabs promised to look after him and feed him well.

One dark night the wicked queen was walking near the lake when she saw a faint silvery light near its shore. She went closer to inspect the water's edge and found the moonprince peacefully asleep but surrounded by solicitous crabs with their pincers up in defence, all alert with their beady eyes open on top of their scaly heads. The queen did not have the courage to go near, on the contrary she ran back to the town and sat down near the king, panting. When the king asked her what the matter was, she said, 'Your Majesty, I am ill, gravely ill. As you can see, I am gasping for breath. I went to see the diviner who consulted his oracle bones and told me that the only cure for this illness was to eat crabs from the lake, as many as can be caught by your fishermen.' The king promised her that early in the morning the lake would be drained and all the crabs caught. She would have them all, for breakfast, lunch and dinner.

Luckily the alert spy-mouse was still sitting

under the king's chair with his big round ears wide open. As soon as he heard the king make his promise, he ran down to the lake and told the crabs what he had heard. He also had a solution to the problem, 'In the town on the other side of the lake there lives a merchant. Take the prince to him. He will look after this handsome boy.'

The merchant was, of course, deeply astonished when he saw crabs knocking on the door of his store. But his surprise grew even more when he saw that they were accompanied by a little boy whose breast shone with bright moonlight. Finally, his mouth fell open with incredulity when the crabs actually began to speak perfectly in his own language. They told him everything that had happened and while he stood doubting, a little mouse climbed up on the shop's counter and started talking in a hurried squeak, confirming everything the crabs had said.

The merchant agreed to look after the prince and keep him in hiding until such time as he could look after himself. And when the crabs explained that they were in danger of being cooked and eaten by the queen, he offered them hospitality in his own pond. The mouse stayed with him, too, to keep an eye on things and the boy began to learn the secrets of the merchant's trade.

Years passed and the queen relaxed: the lake had been drained, the reeds cut and all the fishes eaten. Surprisingly, there were hardly any crabs to be caught, but there was no sign of the moonprince either, so she was content. The king had resigned himself to having a crown prince with only half a moon on his breast although the thought that a prince with a full moon ought to have been born never left him.

One day he heard that a merchant in a town across the valley had a new drink for sale called tea. Curious to taste it, he sent his most trusted messenger to buy some for the royal household. When the king's messenger arrived, the moonprince, who was now a big boy, was having a bath in the shopkeeper's pond, and talking to the crabs who lived in it. To his amazement the messenger saw that the boy had a large disc on his breast which shone like the moon. Pausing only to buy some of the tea he had been sent for, he hurried back to see the king in private.

'Your Majesty.' he said. 'I think you should know (now that you have made the boy with the half moon your crown prince) that there is a boy with a full moon living in the town across the valley. Perhaps I should not say this, but I never attached great belief to the story of Queen Morongoe giving birth to a dog.'

The king regarded this man as his wisest councillor and he thought for a long time before speaking. Finally he said, 'Take me to that place, I want to see for myself; but tell no-one.'

The king disguised himself in some ordinary clothes and secretly travelled to the other side of the valley. No-one recognized him at the merchant's house and he sat down to drink some tea. The tea was brought by a tall boy of grave demeanour who was dressed in a white shirt. (Normally boys in those days had only a loincloth on or a leather girdle.) The king asked him where he came from and the moonprince, who of course did not know his father, told him all his experiences: how the queen wanted him to die and how the mice, then the cow and finally the crabs had each time led him to safety in the nick of time.

'Show me the full moon you carry on your chest,' commanded the king. The boy was reluctant to obey, since it was the moon on his chest that had nearly caused his death four times already.

'Nothing can harm you now for I am the king,' said his father. 'If you have the full moon on your breast, it is God's sign that you are my successor by right. Then you will be king after me and rule this whole country. Therefore show me if you are my son.'

The boy opened his shirt and showed the wonderful shining disc on his chest. The king embraced him and took him home and publicly declared him crown prince and heir to the crown. The merchant was rewarded with the title of royal purveyor. The wicked queen was chased away with her son and exiled for ever. The moonprince's mother was elevated to the position of first queen, and they and their animal friends all lived happily ever after.

The world of the spirits

Everyone dreams and in their dreams sees things they have never seen and visits places they have never been to. Similarly we live and think without knowing exactly how we do it. Many people believe that this is because everyone has a soul, an invisible being living inside the body which visits the places we think we see in our dreams. The soul may travel disguised as another living being such as a fly or butterfly, and can even enter the world of the dead although this is dangerous because once you are there it is difficult to come back. Some people have very strong spirits, and can change themselves into big, powerful animals. In the form of a leopard, a crocodile or a python they can commit the crimes they dare not commit in human shape.

After death a strong spirit will survive its body and move into another. The spirit of a king might come back as a lion or a cobra, and his people will never hunt or kill such an animal even if it takes lives. A mother may return as a cow to protect her child from ill-treatment or danger. People with weaker spirits, for example sickly children, will simply die and never be seen again in any shape or form. What matters most in Africa is the grim determination to live: exactly what we call 'spirit'!

At first, the Yoruba say, there was only Orisha the Divine Spirit. He lived in a house at the foot of a sheer rock cliff and had a slave called Eshu who cooked for him and worked for him constantly. But although Eshu was a servant he was also a deity, the god of fate, and he hated having to serve his master. Finally he thought of a plan to get rid of him. He climbed the cliff and pushed a large boulder over the edge of the precipice so that it fell down on Orisha's house.

Orisha was crushed and the splinters of his house were scattered in all directions, but since he was a god his spirit could not be killed. That is why fragments of the divine spirit can be found in many places, in all living beings and even in the winds and rivers; and that is why there are now 401 *orishas* or gods collectively called *orishanla*, the great *orisha*.

Sorcerers have extremely powerful spirits and perform acts of magic purely for the love of evil, and terrorize entire communities by their spells. Sorcerers can create fetishes (spirits trapped in wooden statues and other objects) and some use spirits to carry them through the air. Many can change into leopards and pythons to devour human beings.

Two brothers were once arguing about the powers of the python and how they would act if they met one in the forest.

'You know nothing about it. You have never seen one and if you did, you would be frightened to death before it even approached you,' the elder brother finally said with a sneer.

'And you don't know *me*,' retorted the younger brother. 'I have never been frightened of anything. If I meet a python I will just slit it open with my knife here. What can it do? It has neither fangs nor claws.'

One day soon afterwards the younger brother announced that he was going hunting. He took his knife, his bow and arrows and went into the forest. He collected pieces of mud with termites inside from a tall termites' nest, covered them with birdlime and set them out in a clearing as bait for the birds. Then he sat down in a nearby hut and waited.

Time passed but no birds came. The day was hot and the man fell asleep. While he was sleeping, a python came lazily sliding out of the bushes and nosed its way silently into the hut. Seeing the man sitting so still, it opened its great mouth and began to swallow his leg and waited.

The young man awoke to find his leg so heavy he could not move it. He looked down and there was the python, its tail stretching away out of the doorway, and its head busily swallowing his leg. The young man was quite unafraid; he simply took out his knife, cut through the python's lower jaw, pulled his leg out of its mouth—and ran away.

He did not go to his hut at once but lingered, talking to his friends in the village, boasting of his courage. There was no sign of his brother and when darkness came, he returned home to sleep. The next morning he rose as usual and called to his brother to wake. When there was no response, he went over to his brother's bed and bent down to shake him. To his horror he saw that his brother lay still, half dead from a great gash in his lower jaw, just as if a knife had cut it open.

The land of the dead

A young couple had been married for a year when the wife said, 'Husband, I want to go and see my parents.'

'Very well,' agreed the man. 'I will go with you to protect you.'

They set off and after walking for a long time came to the bank of a river. On the bank lay a skull which, to their surprise, spoke to them. 'Please carry me across the river,' it said, its teeth and jawbones clattering.

The man did not want to pick it up but his wife said, 'Come, be kind to the poor skull. Carry it across. After all, it can do no harm. Perhaps it lives on the other side.'

So the man, to please his wife, picked the skull up and waded into the river. The skull said, 'Put me on your shoulder,' and when the man refused and tried to throw it into the water, it bit his fingers and hung on to his hand. The man put it on his shoulder, hoping it would release his hand so that he could throw it off but the skull was too clever for him. As it let go of the man's hand it said, 'If you do not do as I tell you, I will bite through your neck.'

On the other side of the river, the skull told them to walk on and they continued in silence until they came to a narrow path leading off the road into the bush. Suddenly the skull said, 'Turn in here.'

'But I don't want to go there, we have to go to visit my wife's parents,' said the man. 'It is getting late, the sun is setting.'

As an answer, the skull bit the man's neck so hard that he nearly fainted. On and on they walked through the bush until at last they came to a deserted village, its huts lying in ruins among the weeds. It was the place where the dead lived.

The man and his wife were soon surrounded by spirits, fluttering in the darkening evening like bats.

'Well done, skull,' cheered the spirits. 'At last we have meat again—and two good pieces at that!'

The skull spoke to the terrified couple in his deathly, rattling voice, but in an almost friendly tone. 'Now you must go and collect firewood.

It's the last thing you have to do for me before you are cooked over the fire. Do not try to escape for we can smell you wherever you are.'

With death in their hearts, the man and his wife wandered off into the forest to collect dead wood. They had no hope of escaping for they could hear the fluttering of ghosts behind them all the time. Then, as they stooped to break off a branch lying on the ground, they saw that a large spider had made her web there and was looking at them.

'Why do you want to destroy my house?' asked the spider.

'We have to collect firewood for some terrible ghosts who are going to eat us,' said the man. 'We do not wish to harm you, but we are afraid of the spirits.'

'If you promise to leave me and my house in peace for the rest of your lives, I will help you,' said the spider and the man and his wife agreed. At once the spider summoned a pygmy antelope and, jumping on its back, called out, 'To the ghost town.'

When they arrived there, the spirits were all clustered around their huts, waiting for the humans to return with the firewood. Before the spirits knew what was happening, the spider had started to weave a vast web all round the derelict huts until the entire village of death was covered under layers of gossamer web. The ghosts trapped inside could not escape and the ones who had been following the human couple became entangled in the web as they flew home. 'Ghosts are like flies,' declared the spider. 'I can easily kill and eat hundreds of them in a day.'

The man and his wife hurried away as quickly as they could, and from that time they and their descendants after them have protected the spider and left her home in peace.

In some stories the land of the dead is a less threatening place, a country where ancestor spirits live a life much like the one they lived while alive and from which they have the power to aid the living.

An old man once cleared a field and planted maize which grew well until one night a porcupine entered the field and ate a great deal of the crop. The following night the old man kept watch but the porcupine stayed away. The next morning he handed his spear to his daughter saying, 'I am very tired. You keep watch for the porcupine tonight.' The girl handed the spear to her fiancé, asking him to keep watch in her place.

That night the young man guarded the maize-field, and soon saw the porcupine. He threw the spear and did not miss: the porcupine fled quickly into her hole in the ground with the spear still sticking out of her back. When the young man explained what had happened the old man said, 'Young man, that was my father's spear—a family heirloom. If you do not bring it back you will never be my son-in-law.'

In the evening the young man climbed down into the porcupine's hole in the ground. He found himself in a surprisingly large tunnel several miles long. He walked a night and a day until the tunnel widened into lush countryside. In the distance stood a man and the young man saw that it was his father, who had been dead

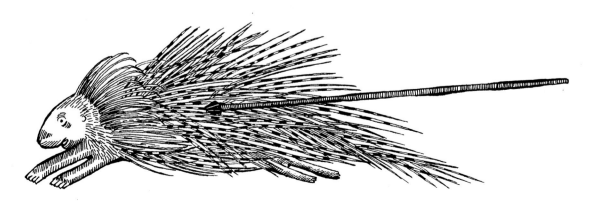

39

for many years; he realized that he was in the land of the dead. He told his father about the spear and the porcupine, and his father said, 'The porcupine that you hit with the spear was your mother.'

'Where is she?'

'In the village over there; you may go and greet her.'

The young man said goodbye to his father and walked to the first hut. Inside he saw the missing spear standing in a corner, and there, sitting on a chair, was his mother who recognized him and asked him for his news. He told her about his fiancée but said nothing about the spear. Then she said, 'I was quietly harvesting maize when I was suddenly hit by that spear,' and she gave him a meaningful look. The young man thought for a moment, then said, 'What do you want from me in compensation? I did not know that it was you when I threw the spear.'

'Put a stone on the fire,' his mother said. 'When it is hot enough I will show you what you have to pay me to compensate for my injury.'

When the stone was red-hot the son suddenly saw his fattest ram appear.

'How did this come here?' he cried. 'I had to walk for a night and a day to arrive here.'

His mother took the ram and asked him if he had shed any tears when he learned that he had stabbed his own mother, and he admitted that he had not. Then she said, 'In that case, sniff this,' and offered him some dark powder. He took a good sniff and sneezed so forcefully that the tears ran down his cheeks.

'Do you like this?' she asked. 'Yes, it is wonderful stuff!'

The old lady rolled up some seeds in a cloth and gave it to him.

'It is called tobacco. Grow it in your garden and sell it to the people on earth so that you will become a rich man. I shall give you this snuffbottle as well. And here, also take the spear back to its owner—it is time that you were married. Now close your eyes and wait as long as it takes to count your fingers and open them again.'

When the young man opened his eyes he found that he was standing in the field of maize

and the dawn sun was just rising. He hurried to his fiancée's father.

'Here is your spear,' he said, handing the weapon back to him. 'And now smell this powder. It was given to me by my dead mother in the other world.'

The old man took a good sniff from the snuffbottle, sneezed three times and decided it was a pleasant sensation. 'Yes, this is very good,' he said. 'You may marry my daughter at once if you give me some of it.'

So the father received the snuffbottle, the daughter married her bridegroom, and the young man planted his seeds in a secret place. They grew well and he was able to sell the tobacco leaves and become a rich man; but only because he had not been afraid to go down into the underworld to retrieve a spear. Tobacco was traditionally used only as snuff by many Africans, who thought it had life-giving properties: naturally it must first have come from the world of the ancestors since they are the source of all life.

The girl and the river god

In ancient times, rivers were often worshipped as gods, because their water sustained the people, their animals and crops. The river Nile was worshipped by the Ancient Egyptians as the source of life, for instance. This story from Mozambique shows the same belief.

The rivers of southern Mozambique are wide and majestic. It is said that they are inhabited by Chipfalamfula, or 'River-shutter', a great fish with power over the water. It can create droughts by keeping the water of the river underground but it is also a kindly spirit and will often help people in difficulties.

A certain chief called Makenyi had many wives. His youngest and most favoured wife had born him two lovely daughters, the eldest named Chichinguane. The other wives envied her position as favourite and they and their children were always unfriendly towards the two girls.

One day all the girls from the village went

out to dig clay for plastering the walls of their huts. When they arrived near the river bank, where good clay was plentiful, the oldest girl told Chichinguane to climb down into the claypit and collect clay for her. It was very swampy down there and Chichinguane had to work standing in the water. She handed clay up to the older girl who filled her basket and set off for home without bothering to help pull Chichinguane out of the pit—although she knew that the girl could not climb out by herself. Chichinguane was surrounded by high walls of clay except on one side where the deep river flowed. The water was rising fast after the rains and before long it was up to her breast. Chichinguane was sure she would be drowned.

Suddenly she saw a huge open mouth under the water. It belonged to Chipfalamfula, the great fish about which she had often heard tales. 'Come, my daughter,' said the giant fish, 'enter my belly and live with me and you will never want to go anywhere else again.'

Chichinguane stepped into the mouth of the big fish and settled down in its belly, which seemed to be as wide as the world. There she found many other people cultivating fields and apparently growing plenty of food. Chichinguane lived inside the fish for many days, lacking nothing.

One day, however, the girls came back to the river bank with waterpots on their heads, singing as they walked. One by one they stooped to fill the pots in the water, then lifted them easily back onto their heads. Among them was Chichinguane's little sister and she was so small that she could not manage her heavy jar alone. No matter how often she tried to lift it onto her head, she could not raise it higher than her knees. What could she do? There was no other way of carrying it and her mother would certainly scold her if she returned with a half-empty jar. The other girls had already left, balancing the pitchers easily on their high-held heads and the little girl sat down by her full pitcher on the river bank and began to cry.

To her surprise she saw her sister Chichinguane emerging from the water, the sister whom everyone had presumed to be drowned. Chichinguane helped the little girl to stand up, dried her tears, then put the pitcher on her head and walked with her towards the village. Before the first huts were in sight, however, Chichinguane said goodbye, turned back to the river and plunged into the water once more.

The next day the girls returned to the river and again left the little sister crying; but again Chichinguane appeared to help her and from then on the same thing happened every evening.

One night the chief's favourite wife wanted to send her little daughter to him with some beer she had made but the pot was heavy and although she tried hard to lift it, the little girl could not do it.
'How, then do you bring me water every day?' asked her mother.
'It is Chichinguane who helps me,' said the little girl.

Next evening the mother went with her daughter to the river and hid behind the shrubs until Chichinguane came out of the water. As soon as she had balanced the pitcher on the little girl's head, the mother came running, trying to embrace her lost daughter.
'No, mother, please do not try to hold me,' said Chichinguane. 'I am a fish now, I have to live in the water.' And no matter how firmly her mother put her arms around her, Chichinguane slipped out of her embrace like an eel and disappeared into the water where she now belonged.

When she was safely back in the belly of Chipfalamfula, Chichinguane began to long for her family and she told the great fish about her mother and sister and how she would love to rejoin them on land. At last the fish agreed to let her go. As a parting present he gave her a magic wand.

When she arrived at her mother's hut, Chichinguane was wearing a scaly fish skin but as she entered she touched it with her wand and said, 'I give you this fish's skin.' Immediately the silvery scales dropped off one by one, turning into silver coins as they reached the floor. With this unheard-of wealth, the mother gave a party to celebrate her daughter's return to the world.

One day chief Makenyi sent the girls out to

collect firewood in the forest and the oldest of them all (the same one who had left Chichinguane in the clay pit) ordered the two sisters to climb a tall tree and cut off branches. When she had gathered as many as she wanted, she and the other girls ran off, without bothering to help the two climb down. The sisters were just testing for secure footholds when a family of ogres arrived at the foot of the tree.

The ogres had human bodies but only one leg each and they were squabbling among themselves. When they caught sight of the two girls, however, they stopped arguing at once and began to chop at the trunk of the tree with an axe. Fortunately Chichinguane had her wand with her and whenever the tree began to tremble and bend, ready to fall, she touched it with the magic stick and the wound made by the axe healed at once so that the tree stood steady and strong again.

After a time the ogres grew tired and decided to rest and rebuild their strength. Soon they were fast asleep. Chichinguane did not wait any longer: she pushed her little sister off the branch and jumped down beside her. They landed with such a thump that the ogres awoke, sprang up on their single feet and started hopping after the girls at a great rate.

The girls ran and ran, hearing the pounding of the ogres behind them, gasping for breath as they went. At last they arrived at the riverbank and Chichinguane touched the water with her wand.

'Chipfalamfula, shut off the water,' she said and at once the river stopped flowing and the two girls crossed over on the dry river bed. As soon as they were safely on the other side, Chichinguane bent down and touched the ground with her wand, singing, 'Chipfalamfula, open the water.'

The ogres were already halfway across the river bed when a great wave surged down and they were all washed away and drowned.

The girls were still some way from home and they had to walk back through the forest to reach the village. On their way they found the cave in which the ogres had lived. Inside were piles of necklaces, beads, corals and bangles together with the bones of the unlucky people the ogres had trapped and killed. Afraid to linger where so many people had died, they put on as many ornaments as they could carry, then hurried on through the darkening trees. When night fell, Chichinguane held the wand high and told it to guide them through the forest. Its tip shone like a flame, lighting the path which they believed would lead them home.

When they came out of the forest, however, they were in a strange place where an imposing palace stood surrounded by a high wooden fence, with guards at the gates. The guards did not see two frightened village girls but two beautiful women bedecked with precious jewellery, carrying a light which glowed mysteriously in the darkness. Respectfully, they invited the girls to enter and offered them a hut and a meal.

'Two princesses have arrived from an unknown country,' the guards reported to the king.

'They must have come straight from heaven,' the king said. 'I was just looking for wives for my two sons. Bring them to me and we will arrange the weddings.'

He could not know that Chichinguane and her sister had been guided to him by Chipfalamfula's magic wand disguised as princesses. And he never knew.

The invisible god

It was a bad time! Bulane, the water god, sent no rain. Gradually the rivers dried up, even the largest ones, all the pools evaporated, the wells contained no more water. The people started digging, following the elephants whose instinct tells them where to look for water in times of drought, in places where there was once a lake or a deep gully in a river. Now everywhere there was just sand.

A certain chief whose name was Rasenkepeng decided he must find water for his people in another country. He sent his most trusted servant, Mapopo, with a caravan of oxen carrying calabashes and other empty containers, food for the journey as well as flour and valuables to exchange for water should they find it. Mapopo travelled for a long time, climbing all the way up a mountain ridge. From the summit, he looked down into a gorge and discovered the shining surface of water. He hurried down towards it and stood at last on its bank. He had knelt down and lowered his head to drink when suddenly an invisible hand hit his face.

Startled, he ordered the ox-drivers to fill the calabashes but when they tried to scoop it up, they could not hold a single drop of water. Then Mapopo prayed to the invisible god of the water, 'Lord, why do you prevent us from drinking?'

'Mapopo, come back with your master's daughter, the princess Motsesa, as my bride and you may all drink to your heart's content. If he refuses, he and all his tribe will die of thirst.'

'Lord, I will give my master your message,' answered Mapopo, 'but please permit us to drink or we shall die before we are able to deliver your message. I cannot answer for my master. I am only a servant in his household.'

The god Bulane agreed and Mapopo and the people with him drank and filled their calabashes for the journey: the water god had to agree that his bride should not suffer from thirst.

Reluctantly, Chief Rasenkepeng agreed to send his daughter to be the bride of Bulane the water god. He gave her an escort and a caravan loaded with gifts which accompanied her far into the mountain valley. There the men unloaded the gifts, said goodbye and returned sadly home.

Motsesa was left alone among the great mountains. As the valleys darkened she looked fearfully around her, wondering where she would sleep for there was no house, no living soul to be seen. Not knowing what to do and growing more afraid as the darkness deepened, she said aloud, 'I wonder where I shall sleep!'

'Right here,' answered a deep voice.

'Right here?' she asked.

'Right here,' replied the mysterious voice.

There was no-one there and it was a long time before she managed to close her eyes for she was afraid of wild animals, of the cold and

of the voice itself. But at last she slept.

When she awoke she found herself lying in a house, in a warm bed with fine blankets, surrounded by dishes of delicious food. She ate eagerly—and invisible hands removed the dishes when she had finished, bringing more later in the day, as soon as she began to feel hungry again. There she lived day after day, wanting for nothing but seeing no-one, hearing only the deep, mysterious voice.'

In due course she gave birth to a son and soon after, the voice gave her permission to return home for a visit. When she came back to the house in the mountains, she brought her little sister Senkepenyana with her as a companion.

Next morning she asked Senkepenyana to watch over the baby while she went to fetch water. While Motsesa was away the baby boy began to cry and Senkepenyana soothed him with a song:

'Little boy, little boy, who has seen your father?'

Next day Motsesa went out again and once more left the child with her sister. Again, when the baby cried, Senkepenyana sang a soothing song to him:

'Little boy, little boy, who has seen your father?'

All at once she saw a tall man standing before her, dressed in a cloth which shone in the sunlight so that she blinked her eyes.

'I am Bulane, I am the father of this boy. Stop your silly song and give me my son. I will look after him.'

He took the baby from her and she fled, terrified.

Motsesa came back with her waterjar and started sweeping the yard, unaware that her sister had disappeared. Suddenly Bulane was standing there, a tall shining figure with her child in his arms.

Dazzled and frightened, she had the courage to ask, 'What are you? Why are you carrying my child?'

'I am his father,' answered a familiar voice. 'That is why I carry him, Motsesa. I am your husband! I am Bulane who opens a house full of dust! One day I will dress my son in metal

armour and he will be a great warrior, a leader of men, a king! I open new ways for people: your father's servants found my well because I led them to it. Now I will show you my city. You have married a king, Motsesa!'

Timidly Motsesa looked around her and saw to her astonishment that there were houses everywhere and that people were walking along with cows, goats, sheep, carrying vegetables to market, filling pots and pans with milk and yoghurt, going about their daily business. When they saw her they all greeted her respectfully, clapping their hands and calling to her, 'Our queen, the mother of our prince!'

And Motsesa laughed with joy.

The orphan and the tree

Once there was a chief's daughter whose mother had died and whose stepmother was very cruel to her. Every so often the poor girl went to sit crying on her mother's grave and one day, when she was particularly unhappy, she saw that the earth of the grave had parted and a green shoot was pushing its way out. As she watched it grew into a stalk with leaves and buds, then into a sapling, then into a tall tree. The wind rustled its leaves and the tree whispered:
'Daughter, daughter, do not cry,
I your mother am nearby.
Pick and eat a fruit or two,
I am always near to you.'

To her surprise the girl saw some fruits dangling from a branch of the tree so she picked them and ate them. They tasted good and she immediately felt better.

From then on she returned every day to the tree, ate its fruit and went away happy. Soon the stepmother noticed that the girl looked healthy - even happy. She did not care for that, so she followed the girl and watched to see what she did. That evening she said to her husband, the girl's father, 'I want that tree cut down. It takes the goodness away from my vegetable garden.'

The father refused at first, for why should anyone wish to cut down a good fruit tree? But his wife insisted and finally, for the sake of peace, he had the tree chopped down.

There it lay, seemingly lifeless, and the girl wept on its wounded trunk. She lay there for some time with her arms around it when suddenly she heard a faint whisper coming from the earth beside it. Looking closely, she saw a lump growing up from the tree roots. It grew and grew until it was a pumpkin out of which a trickle of sweet juice began to fall. The girl licked a few drops from it and found it both nourishing and healing. Now whenever she was hungry or unhappy she returned to the pumpkin for a few more drops.

Soon the stepmother again noticed the girl's healthy looks and before long she had discovered the pumpkin, uprooted it and thrown it on the dungheap. The next day the girl was inconsolable. She was lying on the ground by the grave crying when she heard a faint trickling sound and, sure enough, there was a little stream welling up beside her. 'Drink me, drink me!' it whispered and she put her head down and drank its cool water.

This time the stepmother complained that the stream was flooding the vegetable garden and must be filled in so although the chief refused at first, in the end he had sand thrown into the clear water until the grave was dry and silent.

The girl was sitting crying again on her mother's grave one day when a young man came out of the bush. He saw the fruit tree lying there and decided it was just what he needed to make a bow and arrows. Taking out his knife, he started to carve and, seeing the girl, began to talk to her.
'I am a hunter,' he told her 'and I need this bow and arrow for my work.'
'It is my tree,' she replied, 'it once grew here on my mother's grave.'

They talked for a long time and the hunter decided he liked her so much he would ask for her hand in marriage.
'Very well,' said the father, 'but on one condition. You must kill a dozen buffaloes for the wedding party.'
'If he manages that,' said the stepmother, 'we shall be rich, especially with the girl off our hands, too.'

The hunter had never killed more than one buffalo at a time—that was difficult enough—but this time he had not been in the bush long before he saw a herd of exactly twelve buffaloes resting unsuspecting in the shade. He laid one of his new arrows on his bow and loosed it into the air. The first buffalo sank down dead. He shot a second arrow and another buffalo died; and a third, and a fourth. An hour later the hunter came to tell the girl's father that he could send his men to carry the buffaloes back to his village.

And so the marriage feast was held, the hunter married the girl and took her away from her cruel stepmother to his own house on the edge of the village. The mother's spirit could rest in peace at last.

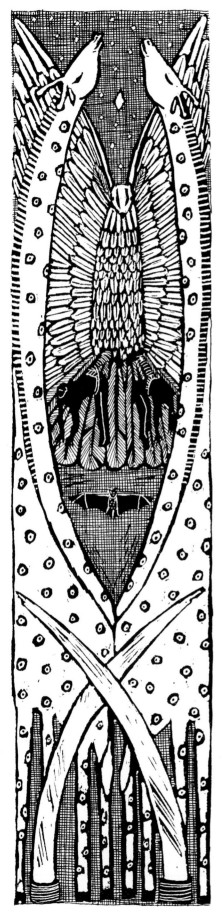

Magic animals

People from every country have wondered about the origins of animals, and in Africa, which has such an immense variety of wildlife, there are many stories that explain their different characteristics. In Tanzania where the giraffe is the national emblem, a story is told that after God had created all the animals, He asked each one if they had a special wish. The giraffe said, 'Lord, my wish is to have wisdom.'

'Well spoken,' God answered, 'and so you will never speak, for talkative people are fools, but silence is wisdom.'

That is why the giraffe sees and hears everything, but never makes a noise.

This is typical of the way African tales serve not only to amuse but also to teach practical lessons. Other animal stories explain the origins of various species, their relationships with humans and their links with the world of the spirits.

There was once a king who stood looking up at the stars one clear dark night. Among all the others one seemed to draw his eye and the longer he gazed at it, the more he admired its colourful splendour.

'If that star were a woman,' he thought, 'I would marry her!'

Later, while he slept, he dreamed he saw the star coming down to him like a white crowned crane onto a lake. The next evening, after sunset, the chief minister came to him and announced, 'There is a lady to see your Majesty. She says you asked her to marry you.'

No-one can describe the king's astonishment when he saw a young girl coming towards him, a girl whose skin shone like the stars in the Milky Way.

'I am Nyachero, the daughter of the star,' she said. 'Last night you said you wanted to marry me.'

'I do,' answered the king when he had recovered his voice. Immediately he ordered that preparations be made for a great feast. 'There must be food for all and everyone must dress in their finest garments.'

The king and the daughter of the star were married the same night.

Now stars have only a night life: in the daytime they have to sleep, out of sight, so Nyachero spent her days in the innermost rooms of the royal palace, only appearing when twilight fell.

After a few months Nyachero said, 'I want to go home now to see my parents and have my baby there.'

The king thought this a reasonable request, for in his country it was quite normal for a young wife to have her first baby in her mother's house. He agreed to give her an escort of twelve armed men and to send twenty-five goats as a present to her parents. That evening, the party set out and wound its way up into the mountains, guided by Nyachero. When they reached the top of the highest mountain, Nyachero called out, 'Father Star! Send me a boat to carry me home.'

Suddenly the men saw the mountain mists as a vast lake and a white boat came sailing towards them. The daughter of the star, the twelve men and the twenty-five goats all boarded the cloud boat easily and it sailed off

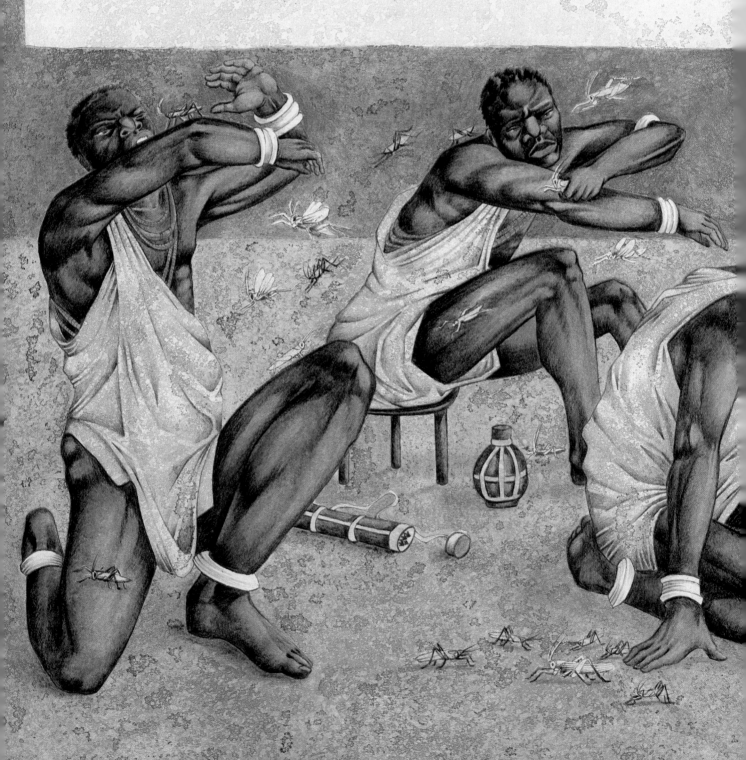

peacefully through the night towards the heavenly country of the stars.

They sailed for many hours and when they finally arrived on the banks of the strange country, there was no-one to greet them. 'My people have gone to dance,' said Nyachero. 'Rest in this house and I will fetch them. You will be comfortable here after your journey. There are beds to sleep on and cool water to drink. Soon we shall bring you food.' Then she pointed to three large pots standing in the corner of the room. 'But remember: do not open any of the pots you see here.'

With these words she left them. After waiting for some hours, the men grew hungry and began to wonder what the three pots might contain. They argued among themselves but at last one man lifted the cover from a pot and peered inside. No sooner had he lifted the lid than a cloud of mosquitoes flew out, whining around them and stinging them everywhere. The men beat the insects off with their hands and sat miserably scratching their skin. However, it was not long before they grew hungry again and someone opened the second jar. Out came a cloud of locusts which flew in their faces and in their hair, crawling over their bodies so thickly that they almost smothered them. Again, the men beat them off and sat down more miserable than before.

Hours later, when dawn was colouring the sky and there was still no sign of Nyachero or her people, another hungry man lifted the lid from the third jar. Out came a cloud of flies which swarmed around them smelling the blood which the mosquitoes had drawn.

All day the men waited in vain—for Star people are never seen in the daytime—and it was not until night fell once more that the cloud boat arrived to take the men back to the mountain top, leaving Nyachero to stay with her family until the child was born. The men saw no-one as the boat sailed under some mysterious power towards the earth—but the clouds of insects they had released from the pots hovered over them and followed them all the way to their own homes. Since then, the insects have never ceased to plague both people and animals wherever they find them.

The buffalo girl

One day a hunter was stealthily approaching the bank of a river, taking care not to disturb any animals that might be drinking there. Good hunters never make a noise in the bush and always make sure they see their prey before they are seen themselves. What this hunter saw as he peered down into the water, however, surpassed all his expectations. Something was certainly bathing in the river but not animals; they were people. Brown, healthy people, big and strong. Where had they come from? There was no village nearby and no sign of any cattle or goats they could have driven that way.

Then, on the sandy banks he noticed a collection of buffalo hides which, if sold to the leatherworkers, would bring him a fortune. Deciding that the bathers must be traders in hides, he crept down along the sand. Still taking care to make no noise, he snatched a hide which, judging from its shape and fine condition, had belonged to a young female buffalo. Just then the bathers began to turn towards the shore and he ran back into the bushes.

To his surprise, when the bathers emerged from the river they walked up to the pile of hides where each picked up a skin and put it on. Immediately each one turned into a buffalo, then walked away and slowly disappeared into the bush. Soon only one young girl was left,

searching anxiously for her skin. Unable to understand what had happened to it, she sat down and burst into tears.

The hunter at once fell in love with her beauty and walked up to her, speaking gently to reassure her.

'Do not cry, lady. I love you. I will build a house for you and we shall live there as man and wife.'

The girl agreed and the hunter did as he promised, bringing her food to eat every day and caring for her well. In due course she gave birth to a son who grew up as strong and healthy as his mother.

One day when the boy was just able to walk, the girl went up the hill near their house to collect firewood. The child wanted to go with her but his father told him to be quiet.

'Carrying firewood is heavy work,' he told the boy. 'She does not want to carry a big child as well and it is too far for you to walk all the way.'

But the boy continued to whine and cry angrily for his mother until the hunter lost his patience and shouted, 'You, a big boy already but still so stupid and stubborn. I can tell that your uncles are buffaloes!'

The boy was quiet after that but his mother was still just outside the house and she heard the hunter's angry words. Instead of setting out at once to collect wood, she searched in the corner of the compound where she knew her old buffalo skin had lain hidden all this time. It was dried and wrinkled but she smoothed it out carefully and rubbed it with special oils to make it soft and supple once more. When she was satisfied with it, she made her way to the hill for the firewood.

At night when she came home the hunter said, 'I should not have spoken like that.'

'I don't want to stay human any longer,' replied the buffalo girl. 'I want to return to the land of my ancestors.'

'I lost patience,' said the hunter.

'It is all right,' said the buffalo girl. 'I am not angry. Come with me and meet my parents.'

Together they made their way to the river bank and there the girl put on her skin and became a buffalo once more. She led him to the place where the other buffaloes were feeding and introduced him to her parents. At first they were suspicious of the hunter but the girl explained how good he had been to her and they accepted him among them. They sewed a fine buffalo skin for him and when he put it on he, too, became a buffalo and lived with them as their son.

From then on their children were born as buffaloes but their first son stayed in the world of human beings; in time he married a chief's daughter and they had many children and grandchildren. Like him, they all had human shape but also like him, they inherited the character of the buffalo and grew up strong, stubborn and ill-tempered; and they never eat the meat of buffaloes, even today.

Two magic birds

There was once a woman called Mamasilo, who went out one day to cultivate a new field. She did not know that this field belonged to a powerful spirit who sometimes appeared in the form of a bird. For Mamasilo the field was just wilderness, weeds and shrubs which she proceeded to clear away with her hoe. She had been working there for a whole day when she heard: 'rrr...' and a bright red bird with scarlet legs and a long scarlet beak perched on a shrub that she had not yet cleared. The bird sang to her in human language:

'I am Senyamafi!
This field belongs to me.
Weeds grow tough! Shrubs come back!
Of the hoeing leave no trace or track!'

At once all the work that Mamasilo had done during the day was undone. The grass she had uprooted with so much effort grew again as thickly as before and the shrubs she had pulled out were back in place, firmly rooted and thornier than ever.

As the sun was setting it was too late for her to start all over again and wearily she returned home and told her husband about the red bird.

Now the bird's name, Senyamafi, means 'Maker of mafi' and mafi is a kind of yoghurt,

made from milk that has been allowed to go sour overnight and eaten with millet porridge as a staple food. When the husband heard his wife's story he made a plan and the next day they went together to the same field. Mamasilo dug a deep hole and her husband sat down in it. Then she refilled it until only his hand stuck out above the soil, and resumed her hoeing and clearing.

As they hoped, just before sunset the bird came back, saw that the shrubs and grasses had once again been cleared and looked around for somewhere to perch. The only thing it could see was the man's hand, which seemed to be growing out of the earth like a branch, so it settled there to sing its song. Immediately the hand closed over it and the bird was caught.

Quickly Mamasilo uncovered her husband and they went home, the man still clutching the bird firmly in his hand.

'I am Senyamafi,' protested the bird in a muffled voice. 'I can make you food. Set me free and I will fill your pots with all the food you need.'

'At home,' said the man. 'We shall go home first.'

Once inside their hut, they shut the door carefully, laid out all their pots and pans, then said to the bird, 'Please make mafi now.'

Immediately the bird filled all the pots and pans with mafi. Mamasilo and her husband were delighted and the husband made a cage, placing it on the very highest shelf where the most precious family possessions were kept. From then on, every night when the children were asleep, Mamasilo would put the pots and pans out ready and with threats and menaces her husband would command the bird to produce its mafi. In the morning there would be food for everyone and soon the children grew fat and healthy, with bright eyes and shining skins.

The neighbours were curious but Mamasilo and her husband kept their secret well and even their own children did not know the source of their food supply. Then one night the oldest son was lying awake when his father threatened the bird. Next day he boasted to the neighbours' children about all the food his

family had in their house and the children all crowded in to see it for themselves. Mamasilo's children allowed them to eat from the pots full of mafi and soon it had all gone.

'Don't worry,' said Mamasilo's oldest son. 'I know how to get some more,' and he pushed the other children out of the hut and climbed up to command the bird to make mafi as he had heard his father do.

'Only if you let me out of this cage for a while,' said the bird so the children opened the cage and the bird flew out and fluttered around the hut for a while. Then it made them some mafi. As soon as it had made enough, they caught it and pushed it back into its cage.

Next day the village children came to demand more food and again Mamasilo's son allowed them to empty all the pots and pans. When all the mafi was finished and the children had left, he shut the door and commanded the bird to do its work.

'Not until you open the door,' said the bird. 'It is very stuffy up here on my top shelf.'

The children did as the bird asked and once again it filled the pots with mafi and allowed itself to be caught—but only just.

The next day everything happened as before. The village children ate all the mafi, and Mamasilo's children commanded the bird to do its work.

'I will make mafi for you but not in here,' said the bird. 'Carry the pots outside to the yard. I will fill them there.'

The bird made its mafi, then flew up to perch on a tree. When the children came near it, it flew to the next tree, then to the next. Mamasilo's oldest son tried to coax it with handfuls of grain but although it hopped near him on the ground it never allowed itself to be caught. Soon, though they cried and begged it to come back, it flew all the way back to the bush and soon disappeared in the thickets.

The children ran into the bush after it and they were soon far from home. They did not notice a bank of heavy thunder clouds building up until suddenly a great storm broke over their heads. It grew dark and before they could find shelter, they were swept into the air by two great talons and found themselves soaring high

above the ground.

The great bird that had snatched them up was called Tlatlasolle and although the children cried and shivered with fright, it did them no harm. Instead, its wide wings protected them from the rain and hail and after a long flight it put them down very gently on the ground in a large field of soft grass. There they found a little hut with comfortable beds for them all—and they were soon sound asleep.

The next day, just as the sun was rising, Tlatlasolle returned and gave them food. They spent the day playing but they could not escape for the soft grassy field where they had landed had high mountains on three sides and a steep escarpment on the fourth. Every day the bird Tlatlasolle came to bring them food and stayed to tell them stories and proverbs, to teach them the names of plants and fruits, how to catch animals for food and how to avoid snakes. The children grew tall and strong, learning all the while from the big bird.

When the children were almost grown, the bird Tlatlasolle announced that it was time for them to return to their parents. This time they were not afraid as he gathered them under his wings and showed them how to hold on tightly to his giant feathers.

Away they went through the air, down from the mountains to the valley where terrified herdsmen scattered at the sight of an enormous bird whirring overhead like a thundercloud. At last the children recognized the trees and houses where they lived and the bird came winging down to alight in the middle of the village. Everyone had run away, of course, but they were all hiding in their huts, peering out and when they saw the strangers emerging from under the bird's wings the braver people crept cautiously out and asked who they were. 'We are Mamasilo's children,' they replied.

When Mamasilo was called from her hut she could not believe her eyes. Aged and sad with loneliness, she had long ago given her children up for dead, guessing that by imprisoning the mafi bird they had offended a powerful and vengeful spirit. Yet here they were, big and strong and healthier than they had ever been.

That night there was a great feast to welcome the missing children home and to celebrate the engagement of the chief's oldest son to Mamasilo's oldest daughter: she was now so beautiful and so wise from all the things she had learned in the mountains that the chief's son had immediately fallen in love with her. The bird Tlatlasolle provided food for all the party, just as the mafi bird had provided food for Mamasilo's family all that time ago.

The origin of elephants

This tale from the Kamba people of Kenya explains where the first elephants came from.

A very poor man once grew tired of his poverty and went to see his witch-doctor to ask for help. 'Go and see Ivonya-ngia,' the witch-doctor told him, 'he that feeds the poor.'

The man walked for a long time until he found Ivonya-ngia in his village surrounded by his cattle.
'Tell me, Ivonya-ngia,' he said, 'how can I become rich?'
'Give this poor man 100 cows, 200 sheep and 300 goats,' Ivonya-ngia told his herdsmen.
'No,' said the man, 'I do not want charity. I want to know the secret of growing wealth—of how actually to become rich.'

The wealthy man thought for a while, then gave him an ointment saying, 'Apply this to your wife's pointed teeth in her upper jaw. Rub them carefully and wait until they have grown. Then sell them.'

The poor man took the ointment home and rubbed his wife's pointed teeth with it. After a few weeks the two teeth had grown as long as an arm, and were pure ivory. The man pulled them out and sold them in the market. After a few more weeks his wife had grown new tusks and when they were long enough her husband pulled them out too and sold them. In this way he became very rich.

His neighbour grew jealous of his wealth and asked how he had obtained so much money. 'Go and see Ivonya-ngia,' said the man. The neighbour did so and also received the magic ointment. He rubbed his wife's teeth with it and she, too, grew long teeth. Unfortunately her husband had not been told that he should pull the tusks out and sell them. They grew bigger and bigger and gradually the woman's face and whole body changed until she became a she-elephant. Finally she burst out of the door, breaking the walls of the hut down as she did so.

In the forest she gave birth to a son who was a baby elephant and they lived together there among the animals. And that was the origin of all elephants, who are still as clever as people.

Mulungu paints the birds

The Yao, who live beside Lake Malawi, say that when the world was new, all of the birds were pure white. Eventually they grew bored with this uniformity and prayed to the great god Mulungu to make them as brightly coloured as the flowers. Mulungu agreed to help them.

All the birds stood in semi-circles in front of Mulungu who sat on his stool like a Yao chief dispensing justice and began to paint them, dipping his painting stick in the small pots of paint that were spread around his feet.

Most of the birds waited patiently for their turn and when each one was called, it would hop onto Mulungu's knee while he selected his colours, decorated it and let it go. However, there was one bird called Che Mlanda who was famous for his restless habits and who was always running up and down the bush twittering loudly as if determined to attract as much attention as possible. Now he wished to be the most brightly coloured of all and did not want to wait for his turn. Instead he continually flew up and down crying, 'Paint me next! Paint me next!'
'Be patient, Che Mlanda,' Mulungu said and continued painting the other birds in front of him in the queue: he gave the bishop-finch its black body and scarlet wings, and painted the plantain-eater in blue, green and purple. But Che Mlanda would not be quiet and kept chattering and calling to be taken out of turn.

Finally for the sake of peace and quiet, Mulungu put down the water bird he was painting and waved Che Mlanda forward with the words, 'Well then, you shall get your wish!' The water bird walked away half unfinished and that is why the Common Stilt has red legs and black wings but otherwise is white all over.

Che Mlanda hopped self-importantly onto Mulungu's knee and the god hastily smeared the little bird all over in a dull, drab brown and dismissed him without another word. That is why Che Mlanda is so drab compared to most other African birds; yet he is still as noisy and fussy as ever, and to this day can often be heard calling out to Mulungu, 'Paint me next! Paint me next!'

Monsters and prodigies

African tales are full of monsters, demons and ogres who frequently disguise themselves as human beings in order to lure their victims to their deaths. Most of these monsters are cannibals and among the most common are the hyena men. Disguised as handsome and tall young men, they befriend young girls and carry them to lonely places where they can devour them unobserved. Fortunately their disguise is not perfect because they have two mouths (one for speaking and one for eating) and the second mouth is hidden under the hair at the back of the neck. The moral of these tales is invariably the same: girls, do not walk on lonely paths and do not talk to strangers. Finally, do not choose your husband yourself but always let your parents select him. Their choice will be a wise one even if, as in the following story, it is a little strange.

There was once a chief of the Basotho tribe who had many daughters but no son. One day his wife gave birth again but it was only an egg, just like an ostrich egg! Nobody paid any attention to it for who wants an ostrich egg laid by a woman? The chief was deeply distressed since he needed a son to succeed him one day as leader of the village but years passed and still he had only girl children.

In the old days it was not unusual for a chief of the Basotho to choose a wife for a son who had not yet been born so when the father of the egg met the beautiful daughter of a neighbouring chief, he brought her home to his village, built her a fine hut to sleep in and sent the appropriate number of cattle to her father as bride price.

The next day all the villagers went to the fields to work under the chief's supervision. By mid-day they had run out of seed to sow and the chief sent his new daughter-in-law back to the village for another basketful of seed grains. As she walked into the deserted village, wondering why she had not yet met her husband, she heard a bumping sound, as if somebody was dancing on his own. When she came in sight of the chief's wife's hut, she saw a huge egg jumping up and down and singing in a young man's voice:
'My father found me a good wife.
Now I will soon have a good life.'

59

For a moment the girl stopped and stared in amazement. Then it occurred to her that this strange bouncing object might somehow contain the secret of why she had not met her husband. She jumped forward to catch the egg and, after a few vain attempts, she succeeded. Was it just her agility or had the egg allowed itself to be caught on purpose?

The girl clutched it to her breast where it lay still, and carried it into her hut. There she rolled it into her sleeping mat to hide it, then locked the hut securely, found a basket of seeds in the grain store and ran back to the fields.
'May I go to visit my father?' she asked the chief. 'I will return before dark.'

The chief agreed and the girl hurried off to consult her father. As soon as they were alone she explained what had happened. He thought for a long time, then said, 'You are lucky that I learned many things about secret medicines from my father. Here, take these herbs and go back to your hut. Now, listen carefully...' and he explained exactly what she must do.

The girl hurried back to her own village and, while the rest of the villagers were still busy in the fields, she began to follow his instructions. She took a pot, filled it with water and boiled it. Then she rolled out the sleeping mat, poured hot water over the egg, rubbed it with suet and herbs and covered it with warm blankets. Next she lay down beside it and stayed very still and quiet.

After a time she heard the egg's voice again. 'I am growing a leg now...now the other one...now I am growing an arm...ah, another one is coming out nicely...Oh! There comes my head at last...my nose now, ah, an eye opens, and another...I can feel an ear now, and the other one!' Suddenly she heard a loud crack as the eggshell burst and when she lifted the blanket she found a tiny man lying there looking up at her.

She lifted him carefully and washed him all over like a baby, then rubbed his skin with oil. She could see him grow stronger and bigger as she did so and she rubbed and rubbed the oil into his fine light-brown skin, until it shone in the deepening darkness; it had taken her all day to make a husband for herself. In that time he

had grown into a tall man.

Now she was tired, so she lay down again beside him, calling him 'my dear Egg'. Her new husband talked to her and they happily went to sleep together.

Next morning the girl did not appear and the chief's wife called to her from outside her hut, 'Daughter-in-law? Are you not getting up? Are you not well?'
'Excuse me, mother-in-law,' she replied, 'I am staying in today, I have a headache.'

The old woman returned with a pot full of steaming porridge and put it down near the door, calling 'Here, daughter-in-law, I have brought you some food so you don't have to cook. If you are not better tonight, I'll come back with more!'
'Thank you, mother-in-law,' answered the girl, trying to make her voice sound feeble and tired. 'That is very kind of you!'

That night, the girl and her egg husband received more food from his mother and they stayed inside, happy together. Next day the girl

The ogre who ate people

There was once a girl who refused to marry. Many young men came to ask her to be their wife but she refused them all. When her parents scolded her for being unreasonably fussy, she simply laughed.

'The young men here are much too ugly for me to marry. Now if a stranger were to come, I might look at him.'

Naturally, the whole village was offended by her remarks and soon young men stopped calling at her home. The girl lived on with her parents long after other girls of her age had settled down in homes of their own.

One day a dance was arranged in the village and young men came from all over the area to take part in it, to show off their skills and strength and to cast their eyes at the unmarried girls.

Among those who came was a tall, handsome young man with hair which grew thickly on the back of his neck. He was at least a head taller than any of the others in his age-group and when he danced, he seemed to leap higher in the air than anyone.

The dance lasted for several days, but however long the dancers whirled, however tired they became, the tall young stranger was always there, never seeming to leave the circle their feet had beaten out in the dust. Only when the girls took their turn did he stand still, watching their gleaming, swaying bodies intently. The girl thought she had never seen anyone so handsome.

On the first evening of the dance, the girl said to her parents: 'That's the man I shall marry.'

They were doubtful. 'Wait until he comes to talk,' said her mother. 'Then we shall see. We need to know more about him. Your father must enquire into it. Let him decide.'

On the second evening the stranger singled out the girl and on the third he came to her father's hut and sat talking far into the night. The girl's father was still doubtful but the stranger had certainly offered a fine bride price—and the girl herself was determined. Reluctantly, the parents agreed to the marriage.

Soon the ceremonies were completed and the

said, 'Egg, you are now big and strong enough to go out. Wear this cloth my father gave me and carry this shield and spear. Go to the village square and sit down on the big chair in front of the largest house.'

The egg man did as she asked and in no time word spread that a stranger was sitting on the chief's chair, behaving as if he were the chief himself. When the real chief heard about it, he hurried over to see for himself.

'What is your name and who is your father?' he asked, after greeting him politely.

'My name is Egg,' said the young man, 'and you are my father.'

At first the chief could not believe his ears and eyes but when the girl came and showed him the pieces of eggshell she had carefully preserved, he perceived the truth and embraced the son he had wanted for so long. In due time Egg succeeded him as chief; and Egg and his wife had many children of their own, both boys and girls, and lived happily together for the rest of their lives.

couple settled down together in the village. For several months all went well. The man joined in all the usual village tasks, treated his wife with respect and fulfilled all the obligations of a son-in-law. Then one day he announced that he wanted to visit his home village, to introduce his wife to his relatives.

Now the girl had a young brother who, though only a child, had his own suspicions about the fine stranger. He begged to be taken on the visit but he was suffering from a bad infection of both eyes and looked most unpleasant. The girl refused to be seen with him.

'What will they think of us?' she asked. 'They will imagine I come from a village of monsters.'

The boy was not discouraged. He simply hid until the couple had left, then followed them at a safe distance until they were too far from home to send him back. The girl had no choice but to allow him to go with them.

The stranger's village was several days walk away, in a part of the country they had never seen before, right on the edge of a deep, frightening forest. However, the relatives welcomed them kindly, immediately gave them a large meal and showed the girl to the hut where she was to sleep. Still ashamed of her brother's puffy, streaming eyes, she banished him to a little shack where the chickens roosted at night.

It was some time before she fell asleep. The floor was hard and uncomfortable and there were a thousand strange noises from the forest. But at last, exhausted from the journey, she slept heavily.

In the very middle of the night the boy woke up with a start. Some noise had disturbed him. Taking care not to send the hens fluttering and squawking from their perches, he crept to the doorway and looked out. There, in a circle in front of his sister's hut, stood a group of very strange looking creatures. He could see that the tall figure in the centre, with his back to the boy, was the girl's husband. But he, too, had changed. Something about them all puzzled the boy and when the moon shone out from behind a cloud, he saw what it was. At the back of the stranger's head was an animal's snout. It pushed

out from the hair at the nape of his neck, its razor-sharp teeth gleaming in the dim light. The stranger was a hyena man!

As the boy watched, the villagers began to march around the hut, loping through the shadows with strange, half-animal strides, chanting softly, 'Eat the meat, eat the meat, but wait until it's good and fat.'

As the first birds began to call, the hyena people stole back to their huts, changing into human form again, hiding their second mouths under their thick hair.

The boy sat down and wondered what to do. In the morning he found his sister sitting by herself under a tree at the edge of the village. He told her what he had seen, but she was too satisfied with the good food she had just eaten to listen to him.

'Don't you see,' said the boy. 'They are fattening you up. You know what hyena people do. They eat humans like you and me. You must listen.'

Since she would not believe him, he offered to prove what he had seen.

'Tie a thread to your toe tonight and I'll take the other end into my hut,' he said. 'Then you'll have to believe me.'

The girl agreed, to humour him. That night he lay awake, watching, and when the hyena people began their sinister chant, he pulled hard on the string and woke her up.

'Did you hear them, sister?' he asked next day. She was too frightened to reply.

Now the boy began to plan their escape, for it was clear that the hyena people would not wait long for their meal. First, he went to the husband and borrowed an axe and a sharp knife. The husband suspected nothing and the boy went off into the forest. Almost at once he found the tree he wanted, cut off a branch and began to shape it into a small boat. When he had finished hollowing it out, he climbed in and chanted to it, 'Turn, boat, turn.'

The boat began to spin round. Faster and faster it turned, spinning like a top, gathering speed until gradually it spun right off the ground. Up it floated, high above the trees and out over the village.

All the villagers ran out to stare at the strange sight and the girl, too, came fearfully out of her hut to see what all the excitement was about.

As soon as the boy saw her, he changed his chant. 'Come down, boat, come down,' and the boat spiralled slowly to earth, landing right in front of his sister's hut.

'Do it again,' cried the villagers. 'Take it up into the sky. Show us how you do it.'

'Quick,' whispered the boy to his sister. 'Climb in. Hurry.'

In a moment the girl was beside him and, chanting his magical song, he urged the boat back up into the sky. Away it floated, spinning round and round as it went. Before the hyena people realized that they had been tricked, it had disappeared over the trees and away into the distance. By the time darkness came rushing down from the hills, the boat was hovering above their parents' own courtyard, spiralling gently down to their home.

Crying with relief, the girl rushed to her parents and the little boy proudly told them everything that had happened.

Some say that the girl remained unmarried for the rest of her life. But others say that in time she forgot her fright, looked more kindly on the young men of her own village—and this time took her parents' advice when she chose her husband.

The bride and the monster

There was once a beautiful girl named Fenyane who lived with her mother and little brother in a house near the river. One day a messenger came to ask for Fenyane's hand in marriage on behalf of the son of the chief of the next village. Fenyane's mother agreed but complained that there was no-one to accompany the bride to her new home, as custom demanded.

'That does not matter,' said the messenger. 'I will hurry on to see to all the preparations and you can send Fenyane when you are ready.'

The messenger set off and Fenyane's mother gathered together her own bridal attire from the corner of the hut: all the necklaces, bracelets, strings of beads, feathers, skirts and bodices, earrings and ornaments she had worn for her own wedding. She gave all these to Fenyane and told her to put them on.

Fenyane was just admiring her new finery when there were sudden shouts from the riverside and some women came running. 'Come quickly,' they called, 'your little son has fallen in the river and the river monster has caught him.'

Fenyane's mother jumped up at once. 'You'll just have to go alone,' she said, running off towards the river. 'Explain to the chief who you are and remember, be sure not to look back on the way. Good luck, good travelling and have a good life!'

Fenyane set out towards the town, also in a hurry, hoping to catch up with the messenger. As she was walking along the path through the bush, she heard a voice behind her, whispering insistently, 'Look behind you! Can't you see the smoke? Your mother's house is on fire! Your brother is drowning! The river spirit has caught him! Your mother is so unhappy she may go mad! She may be setting fire to the house, or perhaps she is setting fire to someone else...'

Fenyane knew that when you are on your way to a new home you must never look back towards your old one; and her mother's words were still sounding in her ears. But the whispering continued and she could not resist any longer. She turned her head to look.

There was no sign of smoke or fire and the village looked quiet and peaceful; but there in the path stood the Moselantja, a monster that looks very like a human being except for its long, long tail. The Moselantja will walk behind you and breathe down your neck on lonely footpaths, whispering lies all the time. Once you have seen it, you can never get rid of it. It will accompany you and insist on one favour after another.

And that is what happened to Fenyane. Before they reached the town, the monster had 'borrowed' her complete bridal outfit and put it on itself, so that you could no longer see its ugly, scaly skin and its long tail was hidden under the colourful skirt. It was especially important to hide the tail, for it had a mouth instead of a plume at its tip and in that mouth were real, sharp teeth! The Moselantja talked and talked, promising to return all the ornaments as soon as they arrived in the town but once they were there, it played a different trick. When they went to the chief's house, the Moselantja took over the conversation completely.

'I am Fenyane,' it said, 'and I am the bride for the chief's son; and this is my maid who serves me. She is a little uppity, she may even tell you that she ought to be married to the chief's son, and not me, but take no notice, maids are like that. Anyone can see, of course, that I and not she, am a worthy bride for a future chief.'

The imitation bride talked with such skill that no-one paid attention to her odd appearance. With her scaly skin and mean little eyes, she was rather ugly, to say the least, but eloquence can make people blind to reality. Fenyane, the real bride, was so modest and bashful that she dared not speak a word and the chief had no reason to doubt the monster's words. So the monster married the chief's son Sopo and a great feast was held in the village to celebrate the event. Sopo took his bride to his own home while Fenyane was sent to sleep in the hut of an old woman on the edge of the village.

The next morning everyone wondered what had happened to all the food left over from the wedding meal: all the unfinished sides of mutton, legs of goats, joints of beef had been picked clean and there was nothing left at all. They did not know that Sopo's new wife had a long tail with a mouth at the end and that it could creep along the floor through the whole house and devour all the food it could find.

Poor Fenyane had cried all night and things were no better in the morning. She was given a scanty breakfast of stiff porridge and sour milk curds and sent out alone to watch the millet. Every year when the millet ripens in the fields, the birds come to eat the grains, so the people have to keep watch. This tedious work is usually left to the girls. They build a platform of reeds to stand on so that they can survey the whole field, and scare away the birds with shouts and menacing movements. They invent songs to keep themselves from falling asleep in the sun and Fenyane, alone, homesick and frightened, began to sing sadly to herself:
'I long for home to see my mother
I came along through veldt and bushes
Go! Pigeon, go!
I thought I came to meet my husband
I hoped to celebrate my wedding.
Go! Pigeon, go!
A monster married my fair bridegroom
I am a servant watching millet!
Go! Pigeon, go!'
I long for home to see my mother
I want to fly over the bushes
Go! Pigeon, go!'

To her great surprise, the reed platform on which she was standing rose up in the air just as if a couple of strong men were lifting it above their shoulders. She was just rising out of reach when the old woman whose hut she had slept in came running to seize the trailing reeds. She pulled it down and spoke gently to Fenyane. 'Don't worry, I know what is wrong. You should be Sopo's bride. You are not a servant girl; and the other bride is not a human. I am old and have seen so many things in my life that I can see things that young people cannot. I can tell an evil spirit no matter how well disguised it is. You don't have to tell me who ate all the food last night. Now listen, I will help you. You have slept in my hut and you are like my daughter. I will go to the chief and speak to him. You stay here and watch for birds a little

longer—and don't fly away again until I come back.'

The old woman went straight to see the chief and his son, Sopo, to explain what she knew. What's more, the wily old woman had a plan ready for restoring the true bride to her rightful position, but she did not tell anybody yet, for the Moselantja had dog's ears, very sharp and well-trained. The old woman persuaded young Sopo to come with her to the fields and to bring with him the messenger, the only person in the town who had seen the real Fenyane. Of course he recognized her immediately. The chief decided to act on the old woman's advice and on her instructions ordered the men to dig a pit seven feet (two metres) deep and equally wide, and twice as long; others were told to slaughter two oxen, four sheep and half-a-dozen goats. The women were told to bake bread, to cook porridge in milk (a great delicacy) and to fry pancakes in fat. Jars of milk curds were placed on the bottom of the pit which was then covered with maize stalks and tree twigs. Fenyane went with the other women to the

forest to collect firewood for a great bonfire.

All this time the Moselantja was sitting by the river, using its long tail to fish for crabs. When it heard the women returning from gathering firewood, it quickly hid its tail and resumed its human disguise. Fenyane had the biggest bundle of firewood and when the Moselantja saw this, it said to her, 'Give that bundle to me. You're only a maidservant and I am the chief's daughter-in-law. I should have the biggest bundle.'

The other women disagreed. 'You lazy creature!' they exclaimed, 'So you think you can just take the firewood that someone else has worked so hard to get together! Fenyane shall carry her own firewood to the village so that everybody can see that she has worked hard. You shall carry nothing so that your husband can see how lazy you are. It's something he should know about you from the start.'

When the women arrived in the village they found the pit with the milky porridge and the jars of curds dug in the middle of the circle of huts. Now there is one thing the Moselantja can never resist and that is cow's milk. So when it caught sight of all that milk where nobody else could reach it, it quite forgot its disguise and its tail came snaking out of its hiding place under its skirt. It was a very, very long tail and it easily reached down to the bottom of the pit, where it began to suck up the milk with astonishing speed. By the time the Moselantja had sucked up all the milk it had swollen to more than twice its normal size, its belly bulged monstrously and even its legs were full of milk. It could no longer walk, it could not even stand. First it sat down, then it lay down on its side, all the time guzzling milk with a thirst like an elephant's. Finally, it sank into a deep sleep, like a satisfied python that has devoured a swine. As the people watched in horror, the chief gave a signal, the men jumped forward, struck the Moselantja with their axes, rolled it into the pit and hastily covered it all up with the maize stalks and twigs.

Fenyane's marriage to Sopo was now celebrated with a feast that the people remembered for a long time, because at the same time they celebrated their liberation from a monster that had nearly ruled them all. Although they did not know it, however, there was still some life left in the evil monster. After a short time a wild pumpkin plant appeared in the sandy surface of the Moselantja's grave; and you can be sure that its spirit was in the pumpkin, waiting for an opportunity to strike.

In due course, Fenyane became pregnant and gave birth to a fine, healthy boy. The whole village rejoiced with her. But some people's troubles never seem to end and evil spirits are not easy to destroy. The wild pumpkin grew bigger and bigger and as it grew to its full size, it began to roll this way and that. Its stalk grew longer and longer until it was so long that the pumpkin was able to roll right into Fenyane's hut. When she was left alone with her little son, the pumpkin bumped its way up to her and beat and beat her until she was bruised all over.

This happened several times until her husband noticed how ill she looked. She was too afraid to explain what had happened so he decided to hide in the corner of the hut one day and see for himself what the trouble was. As he waited he heard a rolling, shuffling noise and saw the huge pumpkin lumbering into the hut and hurling itself at his poor wife. With a cry of anger he leaped out of his hiding place, drew his knife and pierced the pumpkin several times until it lay quite still. Then he pulled it out of the ground and threw it on the fire.

He watched until it was burned to ashes before he was satisfied but even then he had not been thorough enough. The next day the little boy hurt his foot and in the evening developed a high fever. Sopo immediately suspected the evil spirit of the Moselantja was taking its revenge and he searched the mud floor of the hut for some sign he had missed. At last, when he had dug up the whole floor, he found three seeds which had grown poisonous thorns; one had stuck in the boy's foot as he played on the ground and given him his dangerous fever. Sopo picked the seeds up very, very carefully and burned them, taking care that not a single splinter, not a tiny fibre remained unburned. It was only when the ashes of the fire were cold and dead that the little boy's fever abated and peace returned at last to the village.

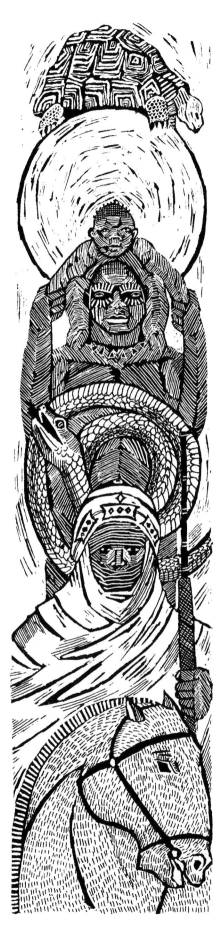

Tales of the heroes

Mokele is the god-hero of the Ntomba people, who live around Lake Ntomba in the primeval rainforests of Zaire: the Nkundo who live north of them pronounce his name as 'Bokele' and his wife's name as 'Bolumbu'. He is both a sun god and the possessor of *kangili-kangili*, a mysterious powder which brings people back to life. From him descended a line of heroes, inventors and warriors whose exploits form an important part of the people's mythological history. This is the story of Mokele's birth and greatest adventure.

Wai was the first man, and he lived near Lake Tumba in Zaire with his wives and servants. One day, he set out on a long hunting expedition in the forest. He said to his favourite wife Moluka, who was pregnant, 'When I come back, I want to see our son already born.' After his departure, days then weeks went by, but Moluka's belly did not grow round. Every day she had to go down to the stream to fetch water, and being very sad she composed a plaintive little song:

'Mother, mother, do you know
Why my baby does not grow?'

One evening at the riverside, she heard a rustling sound and, looking up, she saw what seemed to be an old woman emerging from the reeds. The figure spoke to her soothingly, 'Fear not, wife of Wai. I have come to answer your song.' The old woman touched Moluka's belly and out popped an egg.

'Look,' said the woman, 'this is what you were pregnant of. Give it to me, I shall keep it for you and care for it. Do not forget to bring me food here tomorrow morning.'

With these words, the old woman disappeared and Moluka went home with her water jar, deeply shaken.

The next morning she brought a dish of the finest food to the riverbank. There was the old grandmother, and there in her arms was the most beautiful baby you have ever seen! The woman ate the food which Moluka gave her, while Moluka took her baby and breast-fed him. Then the old woman said, 'Now I must take him away again, but come back tomorrow morning with more food.'

She snatched the baby from Moluka's arms and vanished with him. Moluka went home crying but very early the next morning she

was back at the riverside with another rich meal. The old woman appeared again with the little boy who was now walking beside her. 'Here is your son, Moluka. See how swiftly he has grown. You may take him now, I know that your husband is coming home. But remember, don't show your son to anybody today. Keep him inside your hut until he is fully grown.'

That night, Wai came back from his long expedition and the following morning all the women of the compound came out with their children to greet him. They all laughed when Moluka arrived at the chief's reception-hut without a child.

'You, Moluka,' said the other women mockingly, 'you pretended to be the chief's favourite wife. Have you not born him a baby yet?' Chief Wai felt deeply disappointed with Moluka, and he felt dishonoured too, because a chief expects all his wives to bear him many children.

He was about to divorce her and dismiss her when a noise was heard from Moluka's hut and a male voice rang out, 'Door, open thyself.' The door of the hut opened, and a tall handsome youth appeared. He stood in the doorway for a moment, then said, 'How can I go and greet my father properly? Grass, disappear!'

At once invisible hands cleared a path from his hut to the chief's door. Then the young man ordered, 'Mats, unroll yourselves.' From nowhere mats appeared and invisible hands rolled them out and laid them neatly on the newly swept path. Now the young man strode over the mats towards the place where Chief Wai was seated, surrounded by his wives. 'Good morning, my father, Chief Wai!' he said, 'I am your son Mokele, son of Moluka.' The chief felt great joy at seeing this handsome son and decided to make Moluka his most honoured wife.

In those days there was no sunshine yet, only moonshine, and the people of Ntomba called the moon the sun! One morning Mokele spoke, 'Father, does the real sun not rise here?'
'We do not know what you mean,' answered Wai.
'I will go and buy the sun for you!' exclaimed Mokele, and he started at once to dig out a

canoe from a very large tree. When it was ready, the wild animals emerged from the forest to admire it. First the wasps came buzzing round Mokele's head, whispering into his ear, 'We want to go with you to find the sun. If the owners refuse to let you have it, we shall sting them!'
'Bokendela,' Mokele shouted to the wasps, which means 'Come on board.' There arrived also the tortoise Nkulu, and he, too, asked to be allowed to accompany Mokele to the land of the sun.
'What can you do? You are so slow!' replied Mokele.
'Slow?' wondered the tortoise. 'I am here first of all the wingless animals. I am the Sorcerer of Battle. I will be your War Magician. I can divine where the sun is even when it is hidden from your sight.'
'Good!' exclaimed Mokele, 'Bokendela!' Next, there arrived the kite Nkombe.
'I want to travel with you!'
'What can you do, kite Nkombe?'
'If they refuse to give you the sun, I will pick it up and fly away with it.'
'Good! Bokendela! Come on board! Welcome!'
In this way one after another, all the animals

of the forest were invited into the canoe so that it was quite full. They set off to travel eastward to the land of the sun, and the tortoise stood in the prow of the boat to divine the way ahead while the vigilant kite used his keen eyesight to search for any danger. After a long voyage down the rivers of the dense tropical rainforest they arrived in the country of the patriarch Mokulaka where the sun was hidden.

Mokele greeted the old chief respectfully, then asked, 'Mokulaka, can I buy the sun?'

Mokulaka did not wish to part with the sun, but when he saw that Mokele was accompanied by the fierce leopard, the courageous baboon and all the other animals, he realized that he could not prevent it from being taken. He secretly decided to delay matters until he could get help. 'All right, I shall willingly give it to you, but wait for Yakalaki, my son, before you take it so that we can all decide on a fair price.'

Mokele courteously agreed to this and went away to rest; the old chief at once summoned his daughter Molumbu.

'Molumbu, go and brew poison for these strangers, I want them killed.' He had not noticed that a wasp was still nearby (because wasps penetrate every house) but the wasp hurried off to tell Mokele what she had heard. Realizing that he could not trust the old chief, Mokele decided to carry away the sun by force. However, he pretended to have noticed nothing and followed Molumbu to her own hut. Now Mokele was a very handsome young man and Molumbu could not help liking him. When they had talked for a while, she decided that she could not obey her father and she tossed the poison pot on the floor and sent word to her father that she had gone to the forest to collect fresh herbs. She had decided to elope with Mokele.

Meanwhile, the tortoise had kept his promise. He divined that the sun was hidden in a cave and went to get it, taking the kite with him. The tortoise lifted the sun out of its hiding place and the kite grasped the tortoise in its talons and soared with his burden up into the sky. That was how the sun rose for the first time.

As the sun's light flooded over the forest, Mokele, Molumbu and the crew of animals ran to their boat as fast as they could. The old chief's son Yakalaki had returned by this time and he and his warriors gave chase, but the wasps descended on them like a cloud, stinging them so fiercely that they were beaten off.

Mokele and his friends had many adventures on their way home through the forest but at last he arrived home with his bride. His father Wai and all the people hailed him as the hero who had fixed the point of the rising sun 'up-river' which for the Ntomba people means 'east', since all the rivers in their region of Central Zaire flow from east to west.

Heise the hero

The Bushmen once lived throughout southern Africa, and it was they who made the beautiful paintings which are sometimes found on the walls of caves and rock shelters. As the Bantu peoples migrated from the north, the Bushmen found themselves trapped between them and European settlers in the south, and were forced to retreat into the arid wastes of the Kalahari Desert.

The Bushmen keep no domestic animals and do not grow crops but instead live solely by hunting, trapping and collecting edible insects, fruits and roots. They are expert hunters, and use poisoned arrows which seldom miss. They possess a rich heritage of myths and folk tales, and many of these are about the great hero Heise, who was half-man, half-god. He was a wanderer in the veldt, and he was so familiar with nature that he knew all the animals by name. In those days he had a wife who was a gemsbok, an elegant, grey antelope with long curved horns and black and white patches. He often came to visit her as she was grazing peacefully with her family, and he would bring her honey, a special delicacy. History does not relate whether they had any children.

In the old time there lived a race of men who were called the Eyefooters because they had eyes on their big toes instead of in their heads. This was a very useful arrangement for the eyes could see what eyes in the head cannot. While they were walking, the Eyefooters could see thorns, sharp stones and snakes that would be hidden from an eye in the normal position. And an eye at ground level could also see roots and bulbs, edible lizards and frogs, insects good and bad, birds' nests, scorpions and ratholes.

An Eyefooter named Ikamaega once discovered two sisters bathing in a pool. He stole their clothes, which were lying beside the pool, and hid them in some bushes. When the girls emerged from the water they begged him to return their clothes, but he refused. He imprisoned one girl inside a tree, and was just about to seize the other when Heise arrived. Heise suggested that they should spend the night near the tree that had just sprung up and as the air was quickly becoming cool, they lit a fire. As they were huddled over the fire, roasting some wild tubers to eat, Heise noticed that the Eyefooter was greedily trying to push all the biggest tubers towards him with his feet, on which the eyes were open and alert. Suddenly, Heise took a branch from the fire and scattered some ashes on Ikamaega's feet, saying, 'If you have cold feet, this will surely warm them.' It did. With burning eyes and agonized screams, the Eyefooter leaped up and ran into the pool where he became entangled in some underwater vines and drowned as he could not see with his feet beneath the water.

The next day, Heise was about to set off with the girl when they heard a voice from the tree. 'Please don't go; don't leave me alone; I cannot move; the tree in which I am imprisoned holds its roots in the ground.' Heise then commanded the tree to open its trunk and the second girl jumped out. Both girls agreed to stay with him, so he had two wives from then on.

Another story tells how Heise made the mountains. In the old days there were no mountains, only plains. One day Heise was travelling with his wives and son in search of a new place to live. They had set off early in the morning but as the sun rose over the deserted land, the day grew hot and dry. The little boy started complaining.

'Father, I am only a child, please carry me. I am so thirsty and hot and tired.'

Heise lifted his son onto his shoulders and continued on his way. At midday the heat became unbearable for the sun shone relentlessly down on the parched land. They decided to rest awhile and Heise wanted to put his son down; but the boy clung to his father's fur cap so fiercely that it came off in his hands. With it came part of his father's head and brain, which fell down at his feet. Heise was not at all disconcerted. He simply picked his brain up and put it in his mouth. Then he blew it out, spraying it to the four winds.
'There shall be hills all around us!' he said. Next he took some of his hair and his fur cap and swung these round in all directions, saying, 'There shall be trees and grass on the hills.' And that is what happened! At once high hills surrounded them, sending fresh streams down to quench their thirst, and green trees grew to shelter them from the fierce sunshine. And there in that lovely new country they made their home.

On his wanderings, Heise once met Mamba, king of the snakes and sole owner of all the cattle in the country. The two became friends and Heise asked King Mamba one day if he would give him some cows from his numerous herds. The snake king agreed on condition that Heise helped him to build an enclosure for his cattle. Heise dug in the palissades himself and soon completed the cattle pen. Then he went to ask for his cattle.
'It is cold,' said Mamba. 'Go and collect firewood and light me a fire.'

Heise collected a large bundle of wood and when he had lit the fire asked again for his cattle.
'Let us sit down near the fire,' said Mamba. Heise perceived that Mamba did not want to give him any cows, so he said to the king, 'I invite you to a competition. Who dares to jump over the fire?' And at once, he jumped through the fire and landed unharmed on the other side.

The snake king did not want to be outdone so he wound himself into a tight coil, then darted out towards the flames. Alas, snakes are not intended for jumping and King Mamba's long body fell flat in the flames and was burned to ashes. So Heise inherited all the snake king's cattle, which have belonged to man ever since.

The Dausi

The Dausi is the name of a group of epic songs which tell the strange story of the mysterious city of Wagadu. Four times the city was destroyed and four times it rose again to greatness. Whether built in wood, clay or stone, it always had four gates facing the four directions of the winds; and when the vices of its people became unbearable the city would disappear, becoming visible only occasionally.

The city in the epic is probably based on legends told about the four West African cities of Garama, Ghana, Silla and Agades and when Leo Frobenius recorded it in 1899 and 1915 he realized that he had discovered a key section in the oral history of West Africa. From the names in this epic it is possible to link the history of the Garamantes (who were known to Herodotus and Roman historians) with the mediaeval city of Ghana and present-day Wagadugu. The stories of the four cities may symbolize the migration of the Garamantes from northern Libya southwards to Niger, Benin and Burkina Faso. The following extract is taken from the beginning of this great epic.

The history of Wagadu begins when it was ruled by King Nganamba of the Fasa dynasty. The king was old and frail and his warrior-son, the great hero Gassire, wished to rule in his place. However, the old diviner Kiekorro prophesied that Prince Gassire would never become king but would instead play a lute, and therefore Wagadu would be destroyed.

The prince was furious. 'Kiekorro, you liar, you inventor of tales! You are no sage! How can Wagadu be lost while it has able warriors to protect it?' The old diviner, however, was certain of the future, 'Do not believe me if you dislike my words, prince, but one day you will live among the wildfowl in the fields and will know their cry like a common peasant. And Wagadu shall fall.'

The next day Prince Gassire rode out to do battle with the invading armies of the Burdama who were besieging the city. He fought like a demon and crushed them single-handed so that in the evening the city rang with praises of his bravery and skill. Yet the diviner's prophecy worried him and he went out into the fields to see the wildfowl. A large woodcock was singing beautifully, and Gassire was surprised to find that he was able to understand it. The bird was singing the great epic of the *Dausi*, which Gassire had never heard before, and its words promised that the *Dausi* would live forever.

Gassire's soul was ravished by the incredible beauty of the woodcock's song and in a daze he went back to the old sage.
'Kiekorro! I heard a woodcock singing the great

Dausi. Is it true that it will last longer than the fame of kings and heroes?'

'Prince Gassire, your fate is sealed,' the wise man said. 'Since you cannot become a king, you must become a bard. That is the reason why Wagadu will be lost!'

'So be it,' the prince said and accepted his destiny. He ordered the instrument maker to make him a lute. When it was ready, the prince came and struck the strings. There was no sound: the lute had no voice.

'What is this?' the prince complained to the instrument maker, 'I cannot hear its voice. Make it sing!'

'I cannot make it sing, prince, I have done what I could. It is the best lute I shall ever make. But only you can make it sing. It is only wood. You have to carry it over your shoulder while riding into battle. It has no heart: you must give it your heart. And only living beings have voices. It must drink blood from your blood, breath from your breath. The lute has to hear the cries of battle, the rattle of dying voices. The wood is like the tree it was made of; it only rustles when the wind moves it. The lute will sing when your spirit moves it, when your heart is wounded. Then the voice of your heart, fed by its blood, will live and give the lute a voice! Alas, In that time Wagadu will be lost.'

Gassire spoke, 'So be it!'

He called his eight sons together and spoke to them, 'My sons, today we shall ride into battle. From now on the singing of our swords will be heard by generations yet unborn. Our deeds will be immortal!' Seven days in succession Gassire rode into battle with a son beside him. Each time Gassire fought like a demon and killed hundreds of the enemy. Each time after the battle Gassire carried home one of his sons: young, handsome, and dead; each evening the blood of one of his sons dripped down on the new lute.

The whole city mourned for so many young men who had been slain in battle until finally the people had had enough of warfare. They went to Gassire and spoke, 'Prince, we yearn for peace, not fame. We prefer a quiet life to endless fighting. Go! Take your one remaining son and your followers and leave us in peace.'

The old sage was heard to speak, 'Thus Wagadu will be lost for the first time!'

Gassire, his wives, son and followers rode out of the city and deep into the Sahel, the scrubland near the endless Sahara. At nightfall they rested and all soon fell asleep except for Gassire. Instead he gazed into the flames of the campfire and up at the stars in the lonely night sky. Softly, while all was silent, Gassire heard a voice singing. Was it in his heart? He began to tremble: it was his lute singing. For the first time the lute had a voice and it sang the *Epic of Dausi.* Gassire's wrath vanished. He felt quiet and peaceful. His heart overflowed and tears welled in his eyes. Gassire wept for the first time since he was a child. In that same night his father, King Nganamba, died. But his son would never be king.

Each day Gassire and his people wandered through the endless hills and plains of the Sahel. At night, near the fire, his lute sang the great deeds of the heroes, and everyone enjoyed the beauty of the epic song, the *Dausi.*

Meanwhile, the Burdama had prepared again to attack the city one morning. They were as numerous as before and were a fearsome sight as they approached with the sunlight glinting off their weapons, yet there was no response from the city. The Burdama advanced slowly, then a little faster, and finally they ran towards the city, the men in front being pushed forwards by those behind, and all eager to share in the looting of the city's treasures. No defenders could be seen. No warriors rode out of the gate to face the attackers with their levelled lances. The townspeople wanted only peace.

The Burdama scaled the walls of the city and descended like sparrows on millet. For weeks they plundered and killed: they broke down doors and devoured what they found. When they had done, there was nothing left: no-one alive, not enough food even for a mouse, no wall that still stood. The city was dead. The wind blew sand from the desert into the ruins. At night the owl hoots there before catching a desert mouse. There are no houses. No-one remembers where the town has been. Wagadu sleeps; yet one day Wagadu shall wake again!

Fables from Africa

Fables are stories with a moral lesson at the end. They are a way of saying things in an indirect manner—through them problems can then be talked about without directly offending anyone and advice given in an amusing and memorable way. In present-day Africa this function of the fable is still very much alive, and there are thousands of them. Usually animals are the chief characters just as they are in Aesop's fables. The following story teaches future chiefs how to behave properly.

One day the elephant said to the rain-god, 'You are proud that you make the earth green, but if I tear out all the grass and all the shrubs and trees, there will be nothing left to make green. What will you do then?'

The rain-god replied, 'If I withhold my rain, there will be no greenness anywhere, and nothing for you to eat. What will you do then?' The elephant, trumpeting loudly, tore out the trees, the shrubs, and all the grass, to destroy the greenness of the earth. The rain-god then withheld his rain so that there was desert everywhere. Soon the elephant was panting with a burning thirst: he dug holes in all the river beds but there was no water left. At last, he gave up and prayed to the rain-god, 'Lord, I have sinned. I was proud. I grieve for my sin. Please let rain fall.' The rain-god remained silent while scorching day followed scorching day.

In the end the elephant sent the grouse up to the rain-god to intercede on his behalf. After a long search, the grouse found the rain-god hidden on a remote cloud and pleaded so eloquently with him that the rain-god relented and promised to send some rain. When all the rain had fallen it collected in a pool near the elephant's house.

The elephant went to forage in the forest and appointed the tortoise as his watchman, telling him, 'If anyone arrives to fetch water, say that this is my personal supply and no-one is allowed to take any of it.' As soon as the elephant had gone, many thirsty animals arrived to drink, but the tortoise would not let them. 'This water belongs to His Highness the Elephant; you are not supposed to drink from it,' he said. But when the lion arrived, he hardly listened to the story. He simply looked the tortoise over, then brusquely told him to stand aside and proceeded to drink to his heart's content before leaving without a word. The other animals were encouraged by his example, and came forward to drink.

When the elephant returned, there was no water left. He trumpeted angrily at the poor tortoise for not fulfilling his duties properly. The tortoise said in his defence, 'Lord, I am only a small animal so the others despise me. The lion came and just pushed me out of the way. What could I do? They all drank their fill.' Furiously, the elephant raised his foot and brought it down heavily on the tortoise, stamping on him and kicking him. Fortunately, the tortoise was protected by the shield on his back, which since that day has been flat on one side.

Moral: Do not follow the elephant's example: never defy someone who is stronger than you (like the rain-god); never destroy what you must eat (such as the trees); never appoint a weak person to guard your treasured property; never punish an innocent servant (such as the tortoise); never be proud and don't try to keep everything for yourself—allow others in need to share your good fortune.

The tortoise and the hunter

Many traditional tales support the oppressed, teaching that powerful enemies can be defeated by cleverness and skill.
A certain skilful hunter went out hunting every morning. Each evening he came back from the forest with at least one animal, usually a wild hog or an antelope. One unlucky day, however, he met the Old Man of the Forest, a demon whose name was Claws.
'Ah,' exclaimed the Old Man of the Forest, 'so you are the one who takes all our animals. From now on you will have to share with me. Cut your animal neatly in two halves and give me one half!' The hunter did not like this idea but he looked at the Old Man of the Forest who was twice as big as a human man and was all claws and teeth and he rapidly decided to give up half his supper rather than refuse and be

killed himself. He cut the animal in half, took his share and went home.

The next morning he sneaked into the forest by a little known path, hoping to pass unnoticed by the Old Man. He had no luck: as soon as he had shot an antelope with his arrow, Claws appeared and claimed his share. Again, the hunter brought only half an antelope home. The same thing happened the next day and the next: he could not escape Claws.

Before long, the hunter's wife started complaining. 'In the old days you always brought me a complete animal,' she said. 'Now you bring me only half. I know what you are doing: you have another woman somewhere, and you give her the other half for her family.' 'No!' protested the hunter, 'I have to give half of it to the Old Man of the Forest who is a big, strong demon with many claws and teeth.' 'I don't believe you,' said the woman. 'I am sure you are deceiving me. Whoever heard of such a demon? I want to go out with you to see what you do with all that meat!' She nagged and nagged until in the end the hunter agreed to take her into the forest.

They had only just entered the dark inner part of the forest when Claws appeared. At the sight of his hideous body and his sharp claws and teeth, the woman immediately fainted. As she was lying on the ground, Claws studied her admiringly and said, 'This is the best meat you have brought me so far. Come, what are you waiting for? Cut it in half and give me my share! I have not had anything to eat yet today. Meat is scarce nowadays!'
'That is not meat, that's my wife,' protested the hunter vigorously. 'She's not for consumption.'

The demon was unimpressed, believing that the hunter was merely trying to keep all the meat for himself. 'I know what we can do,' he growled. 'We can ask the advice of one of my friends whose wisdom I have always admired. Lungeater!' he roared and in no time there appeared another demon, more hideous than the first.
'What did you call me for, Claws?' he asked. 'It had better be important, for I am rather busy.' Then he noticed the woman. 'Ah, I am sure, it is this piece of meat that the quarrel is about.

Of course, you know, I must have the lungs before I can give any sound advice.'
'Out of the question!' shouted the hunter in despair, 'this is not meat, this is my wife, no-one may eat her!'
'It appears that there is a problem here, which can best be solved by our capable colleague Hearteater,' said Lungeater suavely. No sooner had he pronounced the name than there appeared a demon even more monstrous than the first two.

Claws explained the problem and Hearteater looked thoughtful. 'Before I can give judgement, or even form an opinion, let me open the breast of this animal and eat its little heart.' When the hunter vigorously protested that this animal was in fact his wife and not food for anyone, Hearteater, after some reflection, replied indulgently, 'If there is a divergence of opinion here, we should of course invoke the help of my learned brother Eyegobbler. He will no doubt solve the matter satisfactorily.' At that moment there appeared a fourth demon uglier than all the rest, with a long bristly snout and small, piercing eyes. He listened to the various explanations and said, 'Of course, I shall have to receive a small fee before I can begin to think about this case. Just let me have the eyes of this animal here, so that I can reflect properly. You will admit it is only an insignificant remuneration for my decisive advice.'

The hunter protested again that the 'animal' they were all talking about was his wife and after yet another conference, the demons decided to call an expert whose name was Bonechewer, another whose name was Skin-tearer, and so on, until the poor unconscious woman was surrounded by more monsters than she had ever seen in a nightmare. Finally, the most senior of the demons arrived: a dignified spirit called Maneater. He decided the case at once by ordering the demons to tie up the hunter and kill his wife. At once the demons began to disagree among themselves about who should have which piece.
'Stop,' said Maneater loudly. 'I will call Ulu the tortoise to divide the meat. Everyone must abide by his decision.'

When Ulu arrived the situation was explained to him in detail, each demon making his own claim for the best meat.
'Well now,' said the wise tortoise, 'this matter calls for serious attention. But first carve with great precision so that my wife can cook *my* favourite piece properly.' The youngest demon swung his knife to cut the woman's throat. 'Don't be too hasty,' cautioned the tortoise. 'Don't you know that women's flesh is unsavoury unless it is properly washed? Did you wash this female?'

All the demons admitted that they had never heard of this preparation of female meat so the tortoise gave them fishbaskets, saying, 'Fill each of these for I shall need plenty of water for washing the meat.'

The demons went to a river which flowed some distance from the forest. When they arrived there, they hurriedly plunged the baskets into the water and pulled them up again, hoping to find them filled to the brim. However, things did not turn out quite as they expected. Fishbaskets are loosely plaited containers which are used to keep fish imprisoned under water, where they stay alive and fresh because the water can flow freely in and out. They were never intended to hold and carry water. But the ogres, who knew nothing of human ways of cooking, fishing and fetching water, filled the baskets and hurried back towards the forest. Before they had even reached the forest edge, the water had all leaked out and they had to return to the river bank to refill the baskets.

While all the ogres were still at the river trying to scoop up water, the tortoise chewed through the hunter's bonds and the man untied his wife.
'You are both free,' said Ulu the tortoise. 'Go home and never come back here again.'

The hunter and his wife needed no encouragement to leave. They quickly ran away before the demons could return and never entered that forest again. But they always remained grateful to the wise tortoise. Even today, the Mongo women of Zaire eat no tortoise meat because, they say, the tortoise saved the lives of the hunter and his wife.

The fox and the crow

Although this next fable comes from Nubia, many of its elements are known throughout the world. Anyone who has read the North American stories of Brer Rabbit will find parts of this story curiously familiar.

A dove had built her nest in a tree and had laid her eggs in it. A fox came along and noticed it; he went home and came back with an axe. 'If you don't give me one of your eggs, I shall chop this tree down,' he shouted up to the dove.

The dove did not want her nest to be destroyed so she threw down one of her precious eggs, which the fox caught and ate. He returned the next day and demanded another egg which the dove was forced to sacrifice. The poor bird mourned for her lost eggs, and a crow who was flying past perched beside her and asked what the matter was.

'Tell me, are your children dying?' she asked solicitously. When the dove had told her about the wicked fox, the crow replied, 'Dare him to chop down the tree — his axe is made only of clay!' The next day when the fox came back, brandishing his axe and demanding a third egg, the dove shouted, 'Go on, chop down my tree then!'

The fox slunk away without a word, because his axe was indeed only an imitation which he had made out of clay from the river. However, he found out who had told the dove about his clay axe and vowed to get his revenge. He lay down beside the road and pretended to be dead. Crows scavenge on dead animals and soon the crow arrived, perched on the fox's shoulder and started pecking. In a trice the fox had caught the crow in his jaws. The crow, however, was careful to remain calm and instead of cawing with fear, she laughed.

'Why are you laughing?' the fox asked without opening his jaws too wide.

The crow answered (after some very quick thinking), 'I had a dream last night, and in that dream I saw just what is happening now. You caught me and threw me up in the air, and as I fell my bones dropped on one side and my flesh on the other.'

'Aha!' exclaimed the fox, 'I shall do just that.' He tossed the crow high in the air, expecting her to fall down, but he had forgotten that birds can fly, and so the crow was able to escape.

A few days later, the fox tried the same trick of pretending to be dead. The crow saw him and landed on his head, pecking away fiercely but still ready to fly away at a moment's notice. Wiser now, the fox remained still, waiting for his chance to seize her. But the crow was wiser too, and she said out loud, 'That's funny, this fox is not properly dead. If a fox is really dead it moves its ears up and down.' At once the fox moved his ears. Whoosh! Away flew the crow in a flash, leaving the fox with a bleeding head.

Moral: It is not an easy matter to outfox a crow! Always keep your wits about you and don't give into threats.

Anansi the spider

Anansi the spider is one of the most popular characters in West African folklore. He is an accomplished trickster although he sometimes outsmarts himself.

The Ashanti say that there was once a man named Hate-to-be-contradicted who was so bad tempered that no-one could live with him. One day he was visited by the small, gentle antelope known as the duiker and the two of them sat together in the shade of a palm tree. Some palm nuts fell and the duiker said politely, 'Hate-to-be-contradicted, your palm nuts are ripe.'

'When these nuts are ripe, three bunches ripen at once,' said Hate-to-be-contradicted. 'Then I cut them down and extract enough palm oil to fill three water-pots. With it I buy an old woman who gives birth to my grandmother, who gives birth to my mother, who in turn gives birth to me. And when my mother gives birth to me, I am already standing here. Now what do you think of that?'

'I think that you are lying,' the duiker said. This made Hate-to-be-contradicted so angry that he hit the duiker on the head with a stick and killed her. Next a gazelle visited the settlement and the same thing happened again. Indeed, many animals paid Hate-to-be-contradicted a visit and he killed them all.

Then one day Anansi the spider visited the settlement and when some palm nuts fell, Hate-to-be-contradicted told him the same tale as before. However, when Anansi was asked what he thought of the story he replied, 'What you say is true. As for me, I have some okra trees on my farm and when they are ripe I join seventy-seven long, hooked poles together but even then I cannot reach them. So I lie on my back, stretch out my arm and pluck them off with my little finger.'

Hate-to-be-contradicted opened his mouth and shut it again before saying, 'I understand. Tomorrow, I shall come and see.'

As Anansi the spider went home, he splashed red palm juice onto the path. Then he told his children, 'Hate-to-be-contradicted is coming here tomorrow. When he asks for me, tell him that yesterday I broke my arm and had to take it to the blacksmith for repair. As he could not finish it at the time, I have returned to have the work completed.'

Hate-to-be-contradicted duly arrived and asked, 'Where is your father?' The children repeated what Anansi had told them and asked if their visitor had seen the splashes of blood on the path. Hate-to-be-contradicted turned red; angry that Anansi was not there to receive him because of this ridiculous excuse. Then he asked the children where their mother was.

'Mother went to the stream today,' they said innocently, 'and her water-pot would have fallen and broken if she hadn't caught it in time, but she didn't quite finish catching it, so she has returned today to do so.' Hate-to-be-contradicted ground his teeth together but did not say anything.

Soon Anansi arrived and ordered his children to cook their guest a meal. They did so but they used only one little fish and lots and lots of hot peppers so that when Hate-to-be-contradicted ate the meal, he thought his mouth was on fire. Turning to Anansi's oldest child he said, 'Get me some water to drink.' The child went away, but returned without any water.

'Where is the water?' the man asked.

'The water in our water-pot is of three different kinds,' the child replied. 'That belonging to my father is at the top, the middle layer belongs to my mother's co-wife, and the bottom layer belongs to my own mother. If I do not take great care to pour the right water, it will cause a serious argument.'

'You little brat, you are lying to me,' Hate-to-be-contradicted cried.

At once Anansi said, 'Beat him.'

'What right have they to do that?' Hate-to-be-contradicted shouted.

'You hate to be contradicted,' replied Anansi, 'yet you yourself have contradicted someone, and that is why I say they must beat you.'

Anansi, his wives and his children beat Hate-to-be-contradicted so severely that he broke into little pieces which scattered so widely that they found their way into everything. The Ashanti say that this is the explanation for why there are so many people today who hate to be contradicted.

The miller's daughter

As with fables, stories that set riddles are popular throughout Africa.

In this story from Morocco, a human is helped to outwit his unjust superior by jinns, a race of spirits in the Islamic world which may be either good or bad. A poor miller's wife gave birth to a daughter named Aisha and then died. The miller looked after the baby as best he could, but he had little hope that he could succeed in keeping her alive. He went to his daily work and did not return until late evening. To his surprise he found the girl peacefully asleep, apparently well fed and washed. The next day the same thing happened. The baby was fed and washed and cleaned, but by whom? The miller had no time to look for the good jinns who looked after his daughter as he was too busy with his mills. No-one was ever seen near the child, yet not only was she healthy and cheerful but her invisible nurses also taught her many useful things so that at seven Aisha knew more than a girl of fourteen.

One day, the sultan decided to test the intelligence of his subjects. He had them brought to his palace one after another, his soldiers picking them at random. The sultan would then ask them to solve an impossible problem: if they did so he would give them a thousand golden ducats but if they could not then their heads would be struck off. No-one had ever succeeded and many heads had rolled off when one day the soldiers arrived at the mill to take the poor miller to the sultan's palace. When he was brought to the royal throne, the sultan told him, 'You are a miller; at the back of my palace garden there is a stream and in it turns a mill-wheel. You have three days to find out what the wheel is saying while it turns round and round.' The miller went home with death in his heart, resigned to the fact that he must put his affairs in order, say his last prayers, kiss his daughter goodbye and that would be the end.

Aisha asked her father cheerfully what made him so glum; she was sure that she could help. 'Have no illusions about that my child, no-one can help me. It is a question to which there is no answer.'
'I know the answer father. Just pretend to listen to the mill-wheel, then recite this poem to the sultan.
I was a tree, I was a quince.
My blossoms spread a sweet fragrance.
Alas, the sultan took vengeance.'

The miller returned to the palace and the sultan repeated his question. At once the miller went to the stream at the back of the garden, pretended to listen to the creaking water-wheel, then came back and recited his daughter's poem. The sultan was deeply surprised. How had the simple miller, who had never been in the palace before, known what had happened? Long ago, the sultan had grown a quince tree in his garden, but one day while he was walking there, he knocked his head against one of its branches. Enraged, he had ordered it to be cut down. The wood was later used for the wheel. Of course, the jinns who looked after Aisha knew all about this and they had told her everything.

The sultan did not show his surprise but said, 'Listen to the next task: bring me a garden on the back of a camel.'

The miller went home in deep despair, but his daughter said, 'It is very simple, dear father. Just wait.' She went out and came back with a flower box. In many parts of North Africa, people grow their flowers in boxes; as soon as a sandstorm threatens they carry their boxes indoors, for if left outside the flowers would be completely covered by the sand and die. All the miller had to do now was to load a box on one of the mill's camels and take it to the palace.

The sultan was delighted but the miller's problems were not yet over. The sultan said, 'Finally, a very difficult problem: next time you must come back riding and walking, weeping and laughing.'

The miller went home certain that this time there was no solution. His daughter, however, saw no problem and explained to her father exactly what he had to do. The next day, the sultan and his courtiers were surprised by a strange sight indeed: the miller arrived seated on the back of a young donkey so small that his feet reached the ground so that he was in fact half walking. He was laughing at his own funny appearance but his daughter had told him to take a pocketful of onions and to continue peeling them until the tears rolled down his cheeks. He came into the garden riding and walking, weeping and laughing. The court burst out laughing at the sight and the sultan had to join in despite himself.

The sultan agreed that the miller, having successfully answered three questions was entitled to the prize of a thousand golden ducats.
'Sire,' said the miller, 'honesty commands me to confess that without the help of my daughter I should now be dead.'
'Bring your daughter here, I want to meet the most intelligent person in my kingdom!'
The miller went home and told his daughter to put on her best clothes, because they were going to the palace together to receive the prize which she had earned so well. When they arrived there was quite a party. The sultan conversed with Aisha and liked her so much that he asked her to marry him, and with her help he changed from the most evil to the most kind ruler that the people had ever had.

The saints of Islam

Today almost 200 million Africans follow the religion of Islam which was first brought to Africa in the seventh and eighth centuries AD. By the later Middle Ages the people had gradually created their own unique Islamic culture and even a special type of Arabic script called *Maghribi* (western). Their scholars were accepted throughout the Islamic world.

There is only one activity that matters in Islam: worshipping God; and only one book to study: the Koran, which is the word of God. The saints of Islam are those scholars and teachers who are closest to God, men who know and understand the Koran and its laws and, obeying it more carefully than others, are almost constantly at prayer. Because the saints are the friends of God, He grants them special favours, enabling them to perform miracles, to conjure food and water from rocks, even sometimes to fly. Among the most honoured of the saints was Sidi Ahmed el Kebir who lived in Algeria perhaps two centuries ago. One day Allah ordered him to go and live in Wadi Rumani, an arid ravine without even a drop of water. It was part of the territory of the Beni Nusair, a proud and impious clan of horse breeders, but as nothing could grow there it was totally deserted. Soon after he arrived, Sidi Ahmed was praying and meditating when a posse of the Beni Nusair rode up to him, stopping right in front of his prayer mat. This was very impolite, because the place before a praying person is regarded as sacred in Islamic custom. The captain rudely interrupted Sidi Ahmed's prayers by shouting, 'I say, holy man, what are you doing trespassing on our land?

Sidi Ahmed opened his eyes and quietly looked the tribal chief in the face. After a few moments he said, 'Peace be upon you, that is how a Muslim greets his fellow-men. What do you want from me, leader of unbelievers?'
'If you can live here, holy man, you must have found water, and it so happens that we are thirsty and so are our horses. Tell your jinn-servants to bring us some water, quickly.'

By this, the chief meant that Sidi Ahmed was a sorcerer who commanded the demons. If the chief had been a believer, he would have known that it is only God who commands the demons.

However, Sidi Ahmed said nothing, but rose, walked to a sheer rock wall that overhung the ravine, and knocked on it with his staff.

Obediently, the rock split and water rushed out, pouring down into the ravine and filling the old dry riverbed. The men drank first, then let their horses drink the clear, fresh water which has not stopped flowing since that day.

Instead of thanking the saint, the chief spoke mockingly, 'Holy man, we admire your witchcraft. Now listen. A wedding has been arranged for tomorrow, but the people have no money for food. We are proud but poor, we need a wedding meal and you will give us one. After that we will leave you in peace to pray to your god in this valley.'

Sidi Ahmed smiled sadly for he knew in his wisdom what would happen, but he promised the captain and his men that he would feed them and their families the next day. He knew that God would provide all that was needed.

The horsemen left to tell their people what they had seen and heard. The next morning all the inhabitants of the adjoining valleys emerged from their humble homes and walked quickly to the Wadi Rumani, which they filled from end to end. Crowded together among the rocks, they anxiously watched Sidi Ahmed who sat calmly in his usual place, apparently unperturbed by the crowds who were hungrily waiting for him to keep his promise.

When all the people of the district were together, and the sun was at its highest, Sidi Ahmed went up to the rock to prepare for his prayers. First he washed himself with the water from the stream God had created the previous day, then he faced east and began to pray aloud. No-one followed his example. After completing his prayers, Sidi Ahmed took his stick and tapped lightly on the rock above the well. Suddenly a large door appeared in the face of the rock. The door opened and out came a big strong man dressed as a cook. On his head he carried a tray upon which was a mountain of *couscous* mixed with pieces of well-cooked meat. Of course the people were disappointed when they saw that there was only one tray, even though it was very big. They grumbled but Sidi Ahmed lectured them with quotations from the Holy Book. 'Did you not hear how the Prophet Isa (Jesus) fed thousands of his followers with a few pieces of bread and fish? Do you not know that food from Paradise will satisfy all true believers without ever diminishing?'

The crowds surged forward and everyone tried to grab a piece of meat, but no matter how he was pushed and jostled, the cook stood immovable, with the tray well steadied on his head. Pieces of meat seemed to appear as quickly as people pulled them out and however many handfuls of the delicious *couscous* were scooped up, the tray still seemed as loaded as ever. After eating for two hours the people sat down to rest, for even the hungriest and greediest do not have bottomless stomachs.

The children of Nusair had eaten more in one day than they had ever had to eat in a week, but still they showed no gratitude. Instead they went away mocking Sidi Ahmed and his 'demon cook', refusing to listen to the word of God. And because of this God cursed them. 'Your cows will not calve nor your ewes lamb!' predicted Sidi Ahmed as the crowd faded away to their homes.

From that day onward, none of their horses ever foaled and no more children were born. Fifty years later, people of another tribe settled in the land of the Beni Nusair whose last survivors were forced to herd other men's flocks.

As for the saint, Sidi Ahmed, he remained in the Wadi Rumani, teaching the word of God during a life of purity and leading hundreds of worshippers in daily prayers.

The haunted well

El-Magharibi was a great saint who never sinned in all his long life. One fine day he arrived in Medea on his way from Morocco to Mecca. The inhabitants of the town flocked to hear him because they knew that performing the prayers under El-Magharibi's guidance earned one's soul a special blessing.

After the prayers the great spiritual guide

Takbou is haunted by an evil spirit, a *shaytan* which takes hold of the water jars and prevents the women from taking its water. I will need seven strong men to help me if you wish me to deliver you from that demon.'

The elders of the town agreed, of course, and soon a line of hefty men had volunteered for the hazardous task of fighting the *shaytan*. El-Magharibi picked seven men who were used to carrying heavy loads and set out with them for the well.

Having arrived there, he stood at the edge of the well and called the evil spirit by its infernal name, known only to the creatures of the invisible world and to those men whom God takes into His confidence. The water began to boil over and suddenly a gigantic horned monster rose out of the pool. The seven strong men jumped back in alarm, but the saint was unperturbed. He commanded the monster to stand motionless on the opposite bank. The monster obeyed and before the astonished eyes of the seven men, it slowly turned into stone, becoming the great rock which can still be seen near that well today.

Quietly, El-Magharibi ordered the men to descend to the bottom of the pool and bring him whatever they would find there. They waded into the pool, but it was deeper than they expected and they had to dive to the bottom. Each came back to the surface with a large earthenware jar with a sealed lid. The sage ordered them to carry the jars to the town's market square where they were opened in the presence of the magistrate. When the mud and rags that had been used to stuff the necks were removed, the citizens saw the glitter of gold. Golden coins filled each of the seven jars; enough to make every person in the town rich! The magistrate asked El-Magharibi to choose what he wished from the treasure but he declined politely, saying that men of God have no desire for gold. All he needed was a little house in the forest to live in. Immediately the grateful citizens set to work and when the saint returned from his pilgrimage his hermitage was waiting for him. He lived there for many years—for frugal men live long—revered by the people as a teacher of great wisdom.

lingered a while in the mosque to answer questions, as is the custom of good religious leaders in Islam. One poor man asked, 'Why is it that our women cannot use the well Ain Takbou which is only a few miles from our town, and why is there so much poverty in our region?'

The old saint smiled knowingly. After a few minutes of silence, he spoke, 'The well of Ain

Symbols in African myths and legends

At the beginning of each chapter the artist has illustrated some of the symbols and characters that appear in the stories.

TITLE PAGE A wood-carver fashions some of the characters in this book. Behind him are a leopard (symbol of royalty) and a giraffe (symbol of wisdom) on either side of a demon and an animal mask. From the left there is a head-rest; a carving of a parent and child to represent the importance of families in Africa; Chichinguane carrying water; an unhappy woman; a fly whisk; the head of a hyena man; the moonprince is suckled by the cow; and a chief's stool that shows a hunting scene. The man is carving a roosting bird which is a common motif in Akan sculpture.

p.11 AFRICA AND ITS PEOPLE A message is sent by drum. Above are the spears and shield of a warrior.

p.15 IN THE BEGINNING The great god of the Bakuba people, Mbombo, vomits up the first things to be created. These included: the sun, moon and falling star; the first man and woman; lightning; the leopard and the tree.

p.28 KINGS AND KINGDOMS A West African king sits surrounded by symbols of royalty. On either side are the heads of leopards, which symbolize the king. Above him is the profile of a queen mother which is based upon a Benin bronze sculpture.

p.37 THE WORLD OF THE SPIRITS At the back the chief's daughter picks the fruit provided by her dead mother. In the middle there sits the man who visited the land of the dead to retrieve a spear—the snuff-bottle hangs around his neck. At the front is one of the single-legged ogres who chased Chichinguane and her sister.

p.49 MAGIC ANIMALS Giraffes, a symbol of wisdom, enclose a scene from the country of the star people while below them are the magical elephant tusks.

p.59 MONSTERS AND PRODIGIES At the top, the monstrous Moselantja wears Fenyane's wedding jewellery. Its long tail which has its own mouth is curled around Sopo the chief's son. At the bottom is the egg from which the little man was hatched.

p.69 TALES OF THE HEROES Nkulu the tortoise locates the sun. In the middle is Heise, who is carrying his son, and below him is the snake-king Mamba. At the bottom is the heroic warrior Prince Gassire.

p.76 FABLES FROM AFRICA The crow perches on Anansi the spider's okra tree while the proud elephant stamps upon the tortoise.

p.85 THE SAINTS OF ISLAM Five holy men stand beneath the crescent moon of Islam. In front of them is the cook who carried the tray of *couscous* and meat on his head and the *shaytan* who haunted the well of Ain Takbou.

Main sources

Amadu, M., *Amadu's Bundle, Fulani Tales of Love and Djinns*, Heinemann, London 1972

Beier, U., *The Origin of Life and Death*, Heinemann, London 1966

Biebuyck, D., *Hero and Chief*, Los Angeles 1978

Bleek, W., *Zulu Legends* (1857) J.L. van Schaik, Pretoria 1972

Callaway, H., *Nursery Tales of the Amazulu*, London 1866

Callaway H., *Religious System of the Amazulu*, Trubner 1870

Chatelain, H., *Folk Tales of Angola*, New York 1894

Doke, C., *Lamba Folklore*, New York 1927

Evans-Pritchard, E.E., *The Zande Trickster*, Clarendon Press, Oxford 1967

Forde, D., *African Worlds*, International African Institute 1954

Frobenius L., *The Voice of Africa*, Hutchinson, London 1913

Innes, G., *Sunjata*, S.O.A.S., London 1974

Jackson, M., *Allegories of the Wilderness*, Indiana Univ. Press, Bloomington, 1982

Knappert, J., *Bantu Myths and Other Tales*, Brill, Leiden 1977

Knappert, J., *Islamic Legends*, Brill, Leiden 1985

Knappert, J., *Moroccan Tales of Mystery and Miracle*, Outrigger, Hamilton N.Z., 1977

Knappert, J., *Myths and Legends in Botswana, Lesotho and Swaziland*, Brill, Leiden 1985

Knappert, J., *Myths and Legends of the Congo*, Heinemann, London 1971

Knappert, J., *Myths and Legends of the Swahili*, Heinemann, London 1970

Knappert, J., *Namibia: Land of Peoples, Myths and Fables*, Brill, Leiden 1981

Lindblom, G., *Kamba Tales*, Leipzig 1935

Norris, H.T., *Saharan Myth and Saga*, Clarendon press, Oxford 1972

Parrinder, G., *African Mythology*, Hamlyn, London 1967

Postma, M., *Tales from the Basotho*, Austin, Texas 1974

Rattray, R.S., *Akan-Ashanti Folk Tales*, OUP, Oxford 1930

Rattray, R.S., *Hausa Folklore*, Oxford 1913

Roscoe, J., *The Baganda*, London 1911

Routledge. W.S., *With a Prehistoric People*, Edward Arnold, London 1910

Seitel, P., *See So That We May See*, Indiana Univ. Press, Bloomington 1980

Umeasiegbu, R.N., *The Way We Lived*, Heinemann, London 1969

Werner, A., *Myths and Legends of the Bantu*, Harrap, London 1933.

Index